THE PAINTED ORCHESTRA

THE PAINTED ORCHESTRA

E. GORDON-WERNER

The Painted Orchestra v.2

ISBN: 978-0-6458971-8-0

DEDICATION

To musicians, bringing joy to life.

Acknowledgements:

With grateful thanks to all the musicians who allowed themselves to be sketched while rehearsing and especially to Richard Tognetti who enabled access

A Note from the Artist

My journey painting Australian Chamber Orchestra (ACO) musicians began when I painted a portrait of Helena Rathbone, Principal Second Violinist with the ACO, to enter into the Archibald prize in Sydney. The Archibald Prize is an Australian portrait prize that attracts many entries from all over the country and generates a great deal of commentary. This portrait led to several other portraits of ACO members as well as many sketches of this group of musical wizards when they were the resident orchestra at the Maribor Music Festival in Slovenia.

I've included the portrait preparatory sketches in this compilation of paintings, partly because they show the artistic process but also because they themselves tell stories about the lives of this group of extraordinary musicians who live to play and who travel the world bringing joy to their appreciative audiences.

When the pandemic hit and travel was suspended, my sketches provided the basis for a series of abstract works featuring members of the orchestra.

The sketches and paintings in this book are being sold in support of the ACO school music program which provides resources and free lessons to disadvantaged schoolchildren who would otherwise not have the benefits of a musical education. Contact the artist at www.artsmitten.com

Elizabeth Gordon-Werner
2024

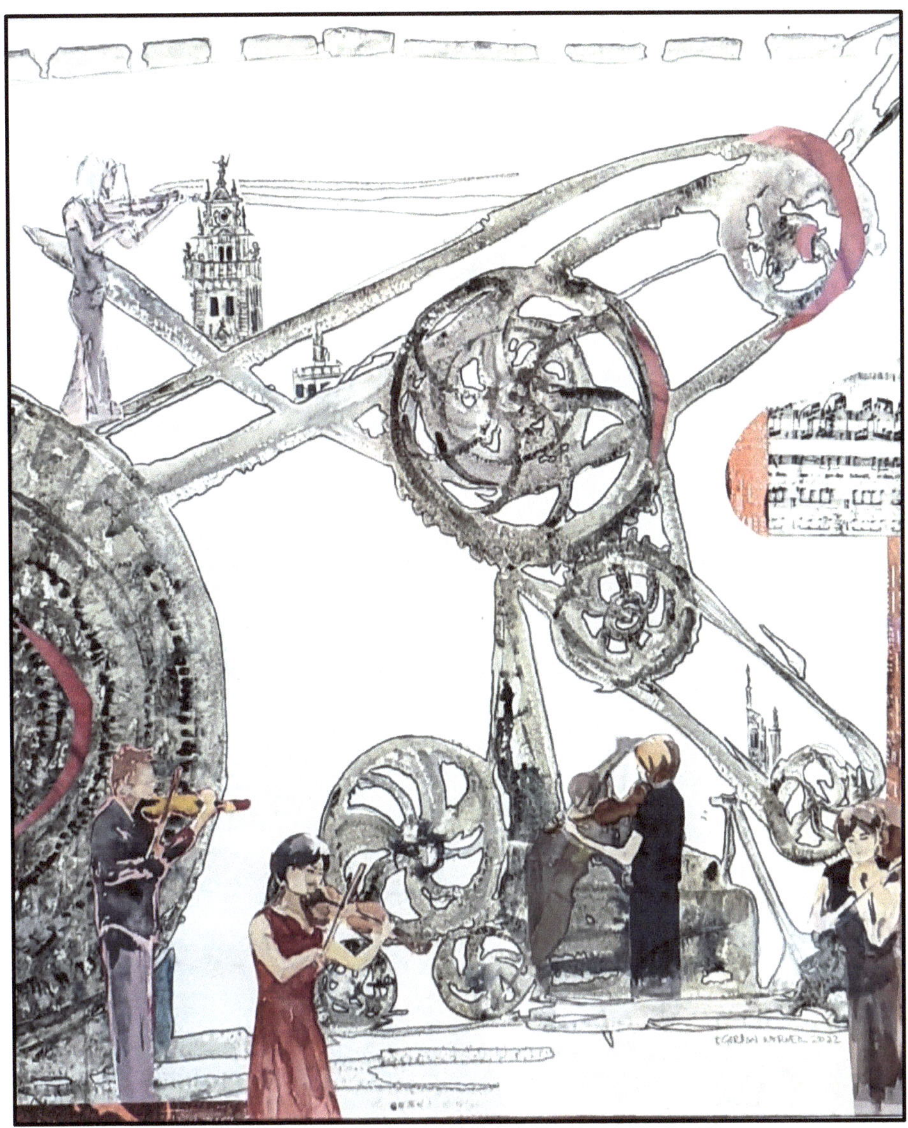

Figure 1. #3098. Music Machine. Collage. 65 x 80cm. Watercolour and ink on Paper.

Painting Helena Rathbone

In 2006, after having had my work hung in several high-profile exhibitions in Sydney I was keen to enter the Archibald Prize for Portraiture, a prize that attracts hundreds of entries from across Australia, of which only about 40 are hung.

The organisers prefer entries of works of people 'well known in the arts or letters'. When I discovered that my subscription buddy to the Australian Chamber Orchestra (ACO) concert series in Sydney worked with the husband of Helena Rathbone, Principal Second Violin, I decided to ask her to be my subject. Helena consented and invited me to a rehearsal to make preparatory sketches.

Drawing musicians while they play is both exhilarating and exhausting. Exhilarating because of the music, exhausting because of the concentration you need to sketch a moving subject. I spent the day in the ACO rehearsal room making quick watercolour sketches of Helena as she played. Then I took a few photos before returning to my studio to paint.

During that sketching session I fell in love, both with the orchestra and with the act of sketching while listening to their wonderful music.

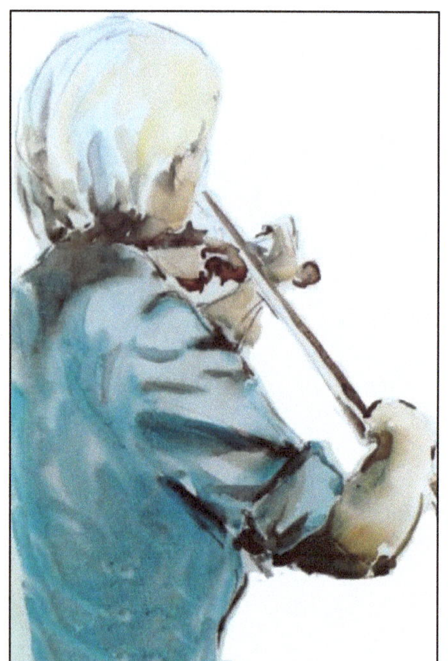

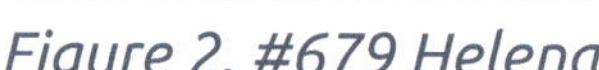

Figure 2. #679 Helena

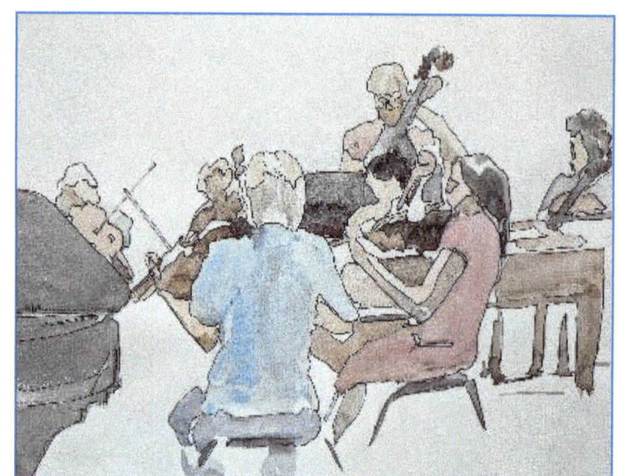

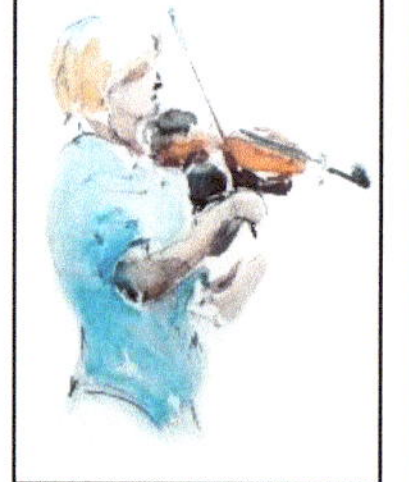

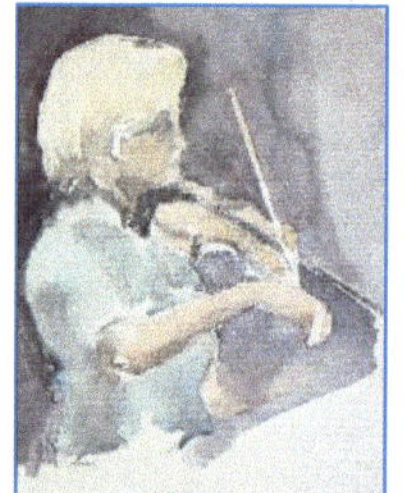

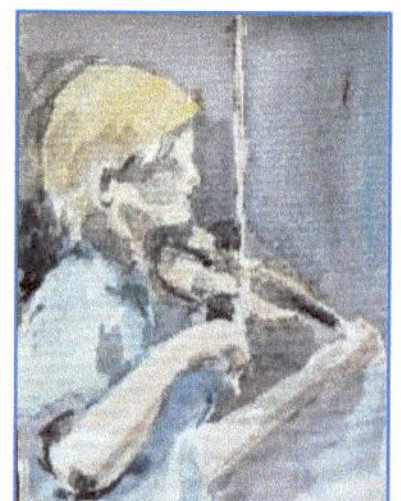

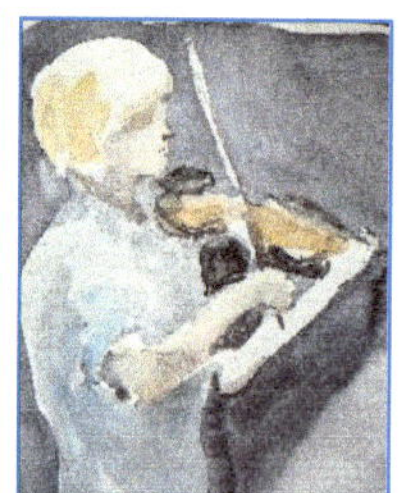

Figure 3 Sketches of Helena

Sketching session

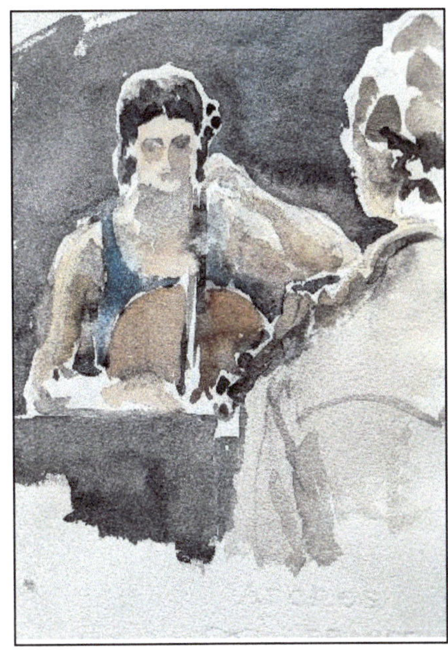

Figure 4. #682 Emma-Jane Murphy

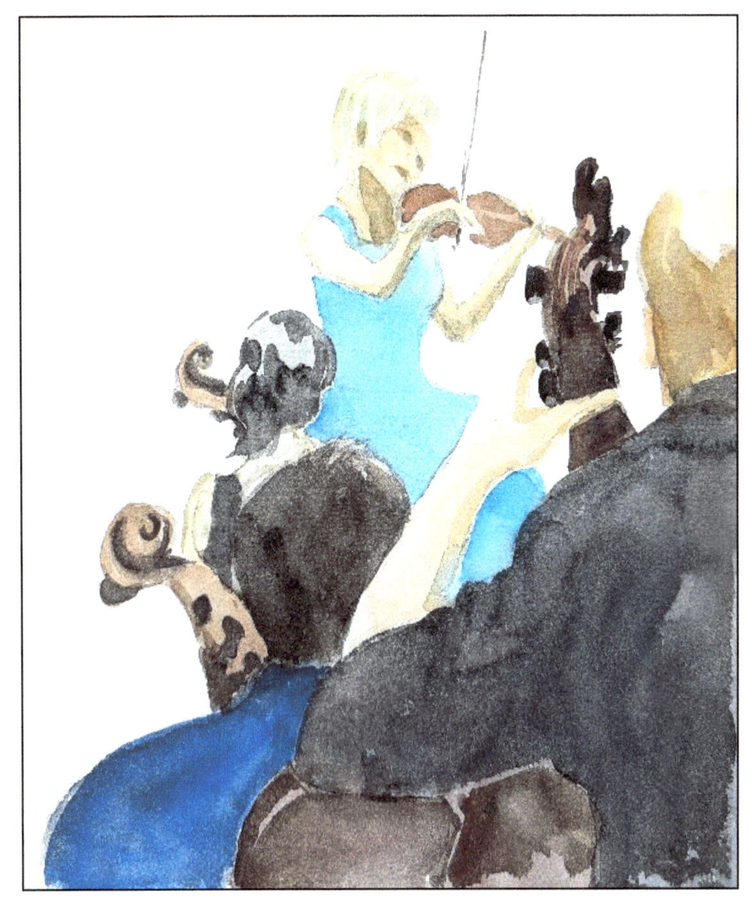

Figure 8. #591

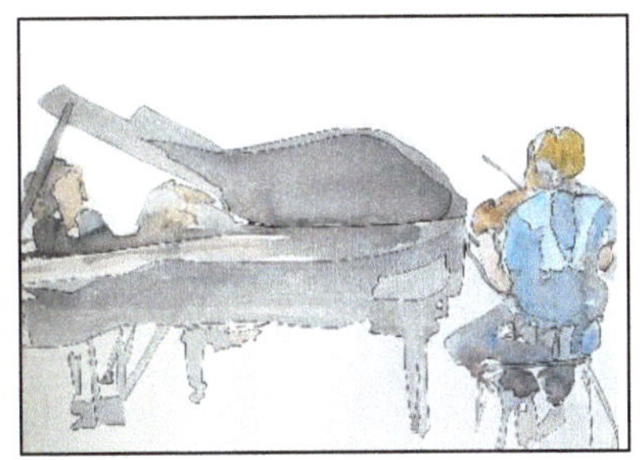

Figure 10. #592

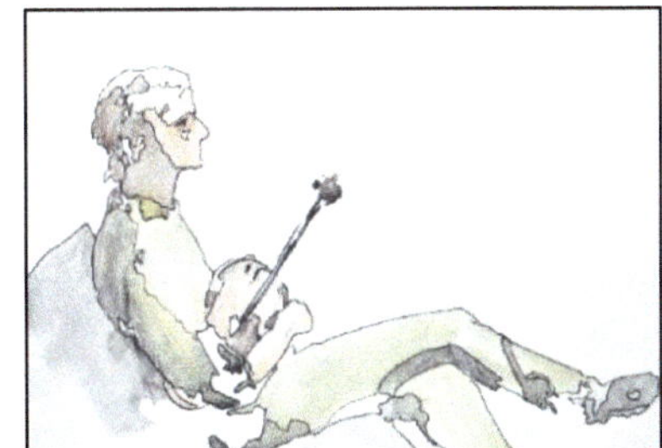

Figure 9. #684

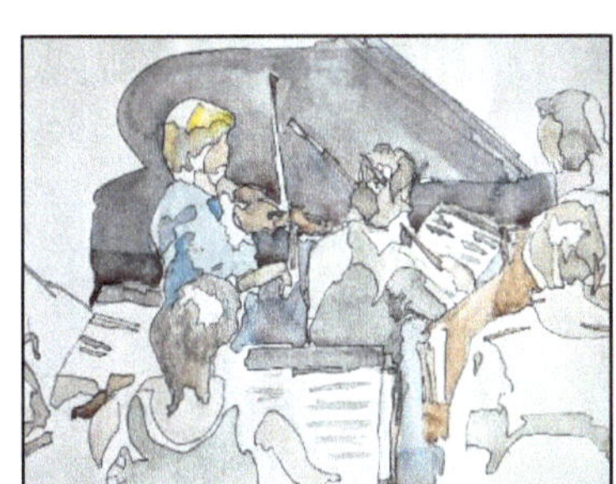

Figure 7. #678

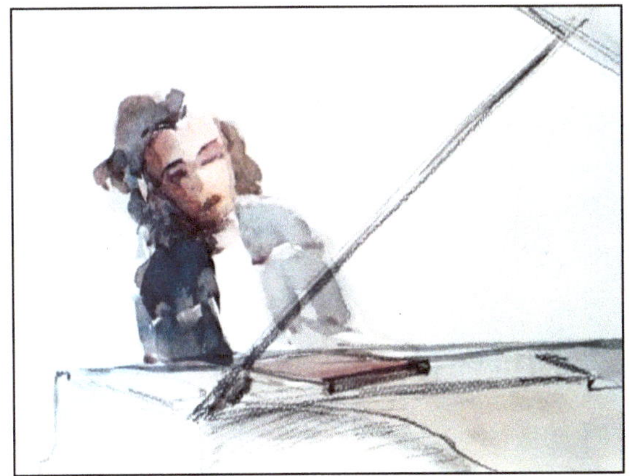

Figure 6. #676 Angela Hewitt

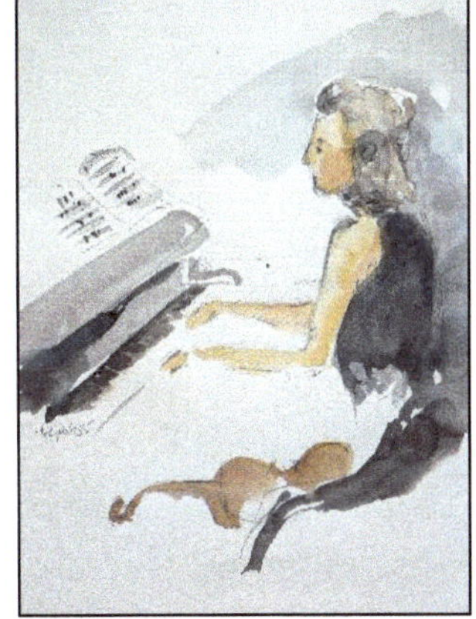

Figure 5. #688

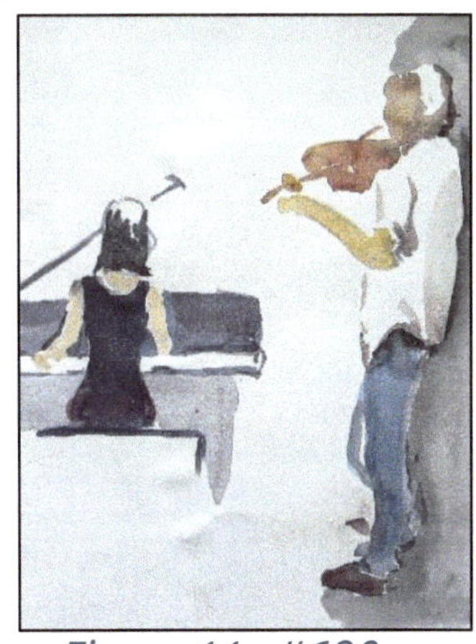

Figure 11. #680

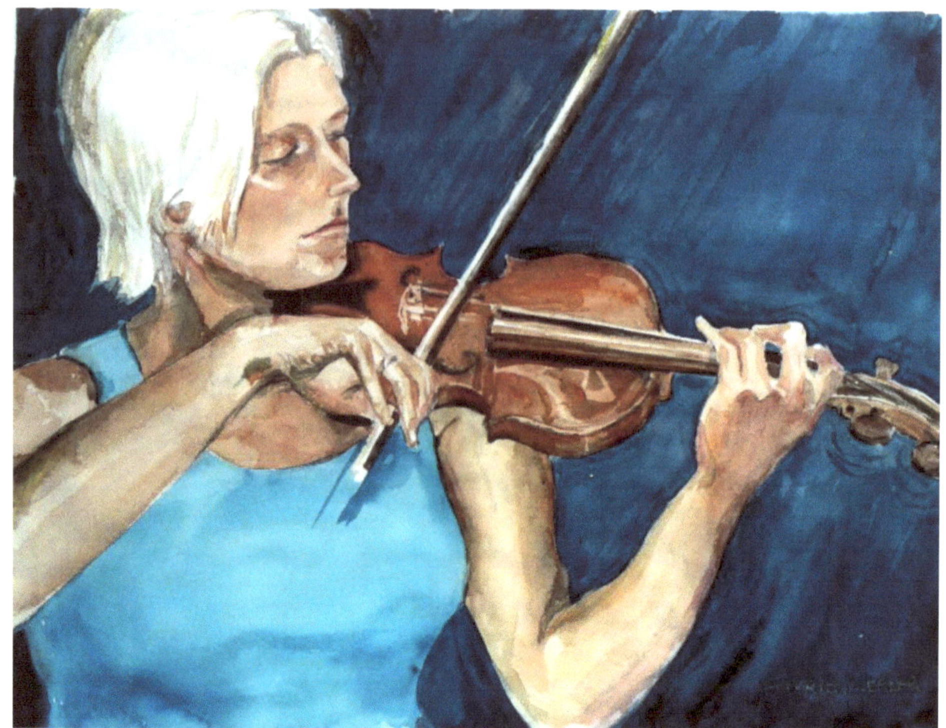

Figure 13. #694 Helena II. 2006. 76x56cm Watercolour on Arches Paper.

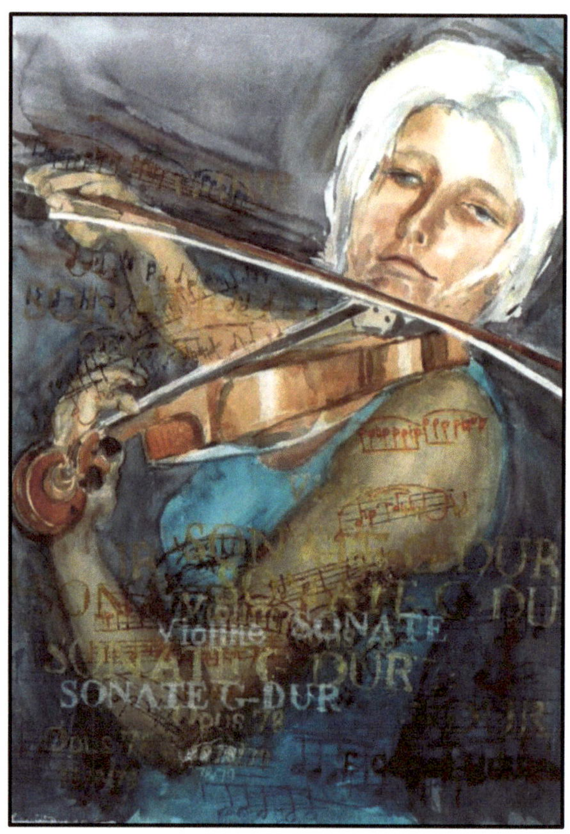

Figure 12.#695 Helena III. 2006. Watercolour and oil pencil on Arches Paper. 76x56cm

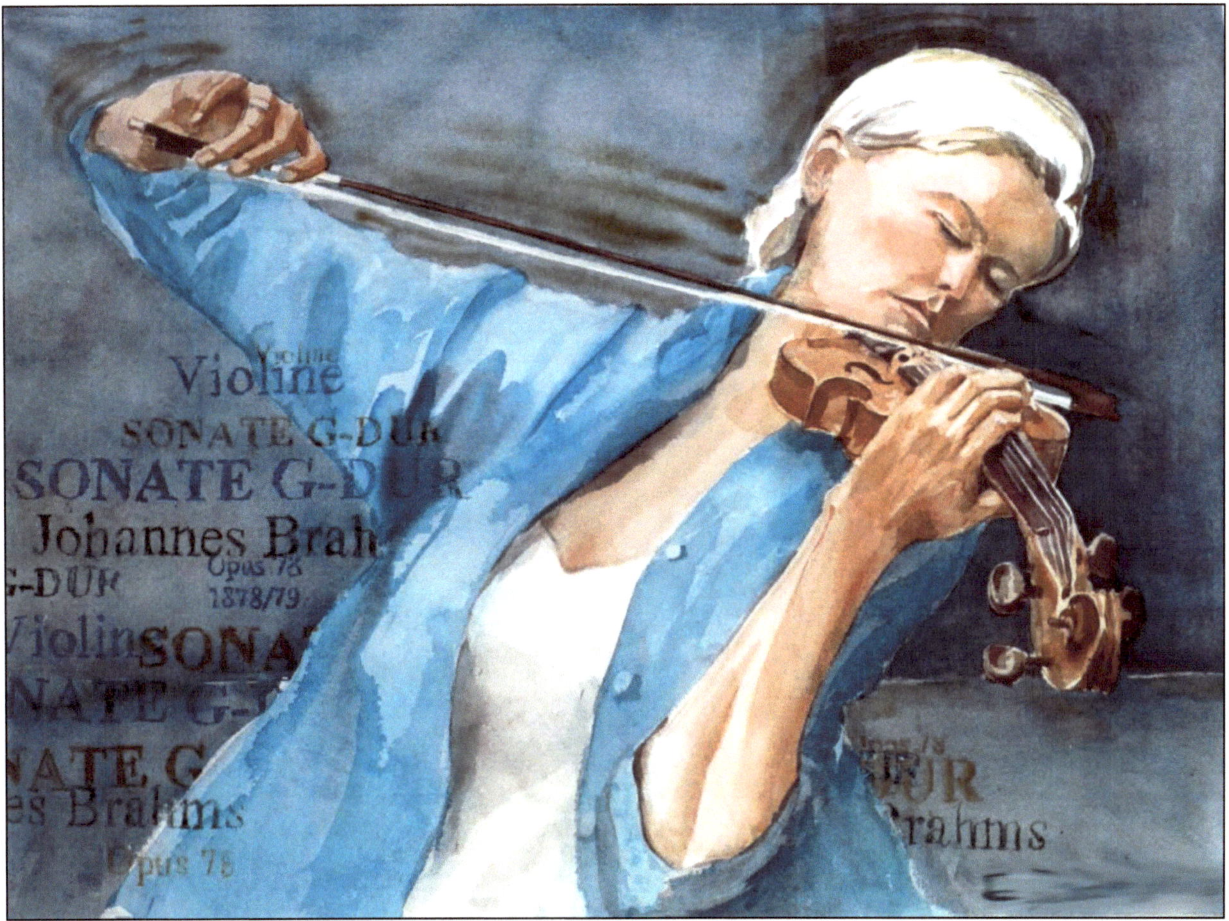

Figure 14. #693 Helena. 2006. Watercolour and oil pencil on Arches Paper. 76x56cm (Archibald Prize entry.)

The music stayed with me as I worked on a series of large watercolour portraits, one of which I would enter for the prize. When I had finished them I asked Helena, her husband and my subscription friend to come for afternoon tea to see the portraits.

Artists capture a moment in time while at the same time attempting to portray something of their subject's character and it is very common for subjects not to like their portraits because they don't see the image that is reflected in their mirror.

When she saw her portrait Helena said, "I don't look like that!"

Her husband's immediate response was, "Oh yes you do! You just don't see yourself when you play."

Next day Helena sent me a photograph taken when she was 14, playing a violin while sitting on the back of a boat. Her stance was exactly like the one I had painted for my Archibald entry. I took her email as acknowledgement that she did indeed look like that.

Aiko Goto: I just love rehearsing

The following year I asked Helena's good friend Aiko if she would consent to being painted. Aiko also plays violin with the Australian Chamber Orchestra.

Aiko arranged for me to sketch as she rehearsed for an upcoming solo concert. She was alone in the room and had been rehearsing for some time when I arrived. I spent a whole long afternoon making quick little sketches while she played.

At dusk, I sat back exhausted and as she packed up her instrument, she turned to me with shining eyes and said," I just love rehearsing! It brings me so much joy!"

Aiko is the grandniece of the famous teacher Suzuki and says that she knew him but was not taught by him. Perhaps her famous granduncle was equally enraptured by the instrument, and this was what he was able to impart to his students.

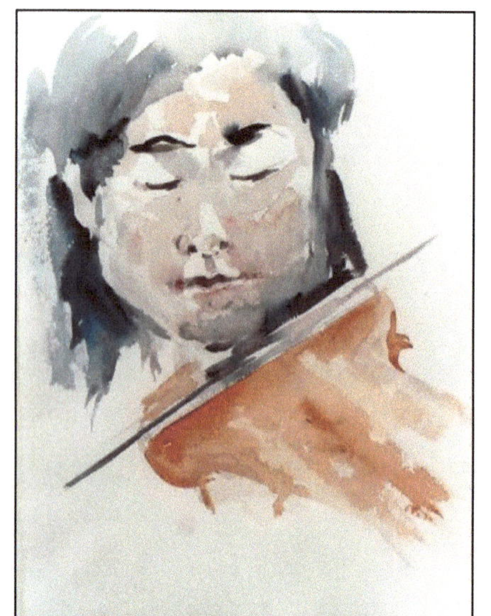

Figure 15 #768

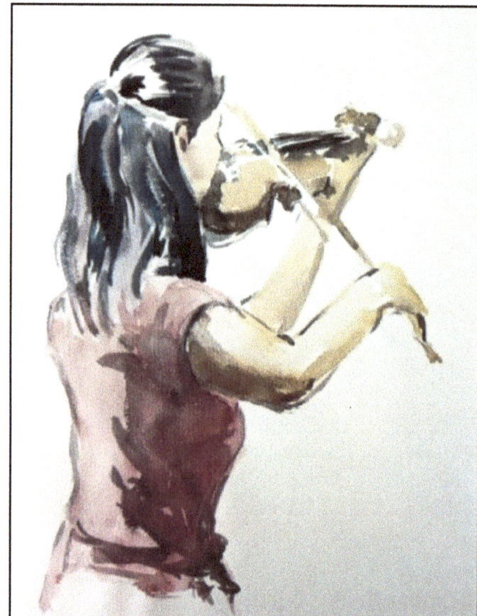

Figure 22. #772

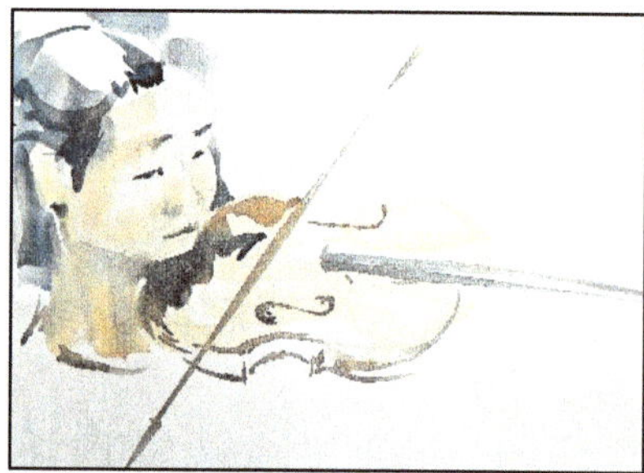

Figure 20 #765

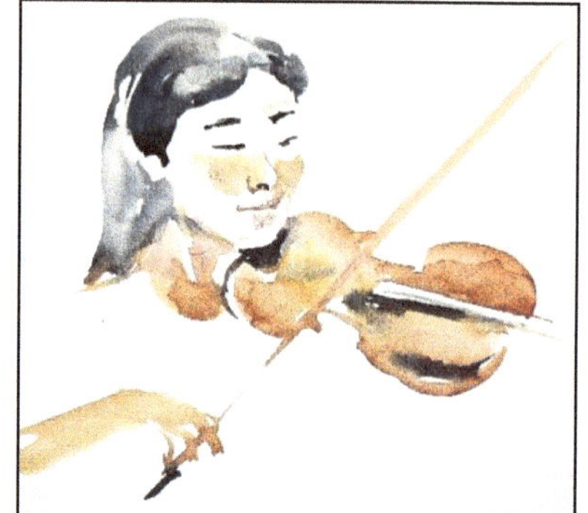

Figure 18 #779

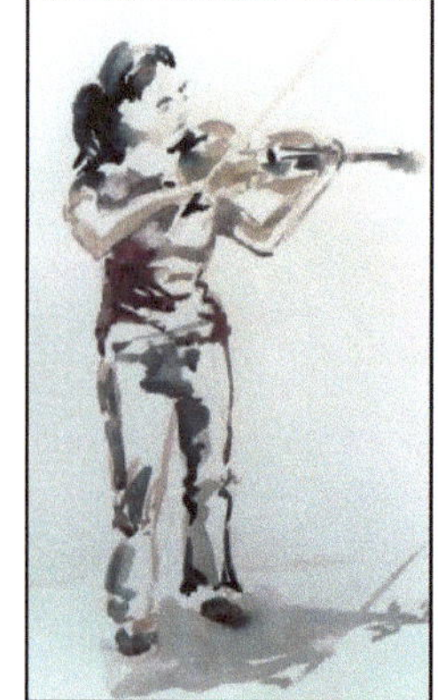

Figure 17. #769

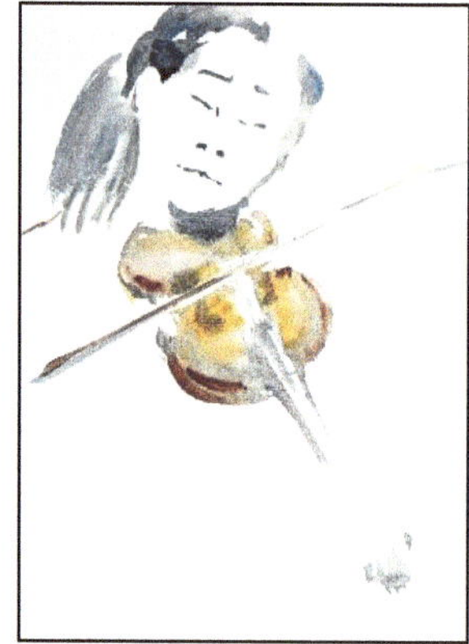

Figure 23. #764

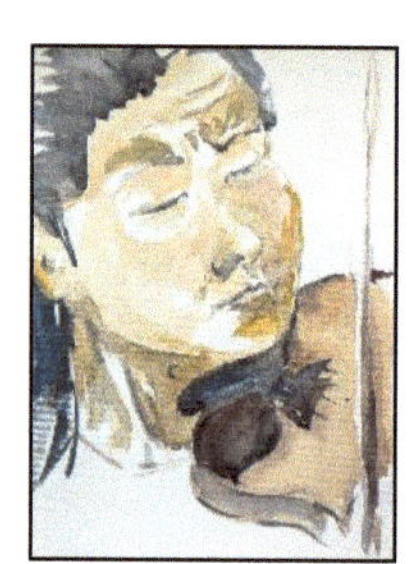

Figure 19. #770

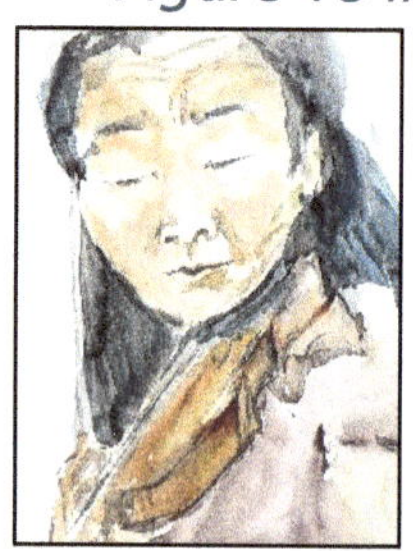

Figure 21 #767

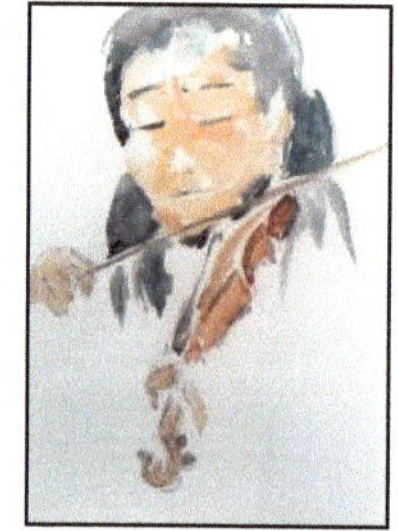

Figure 16 #771

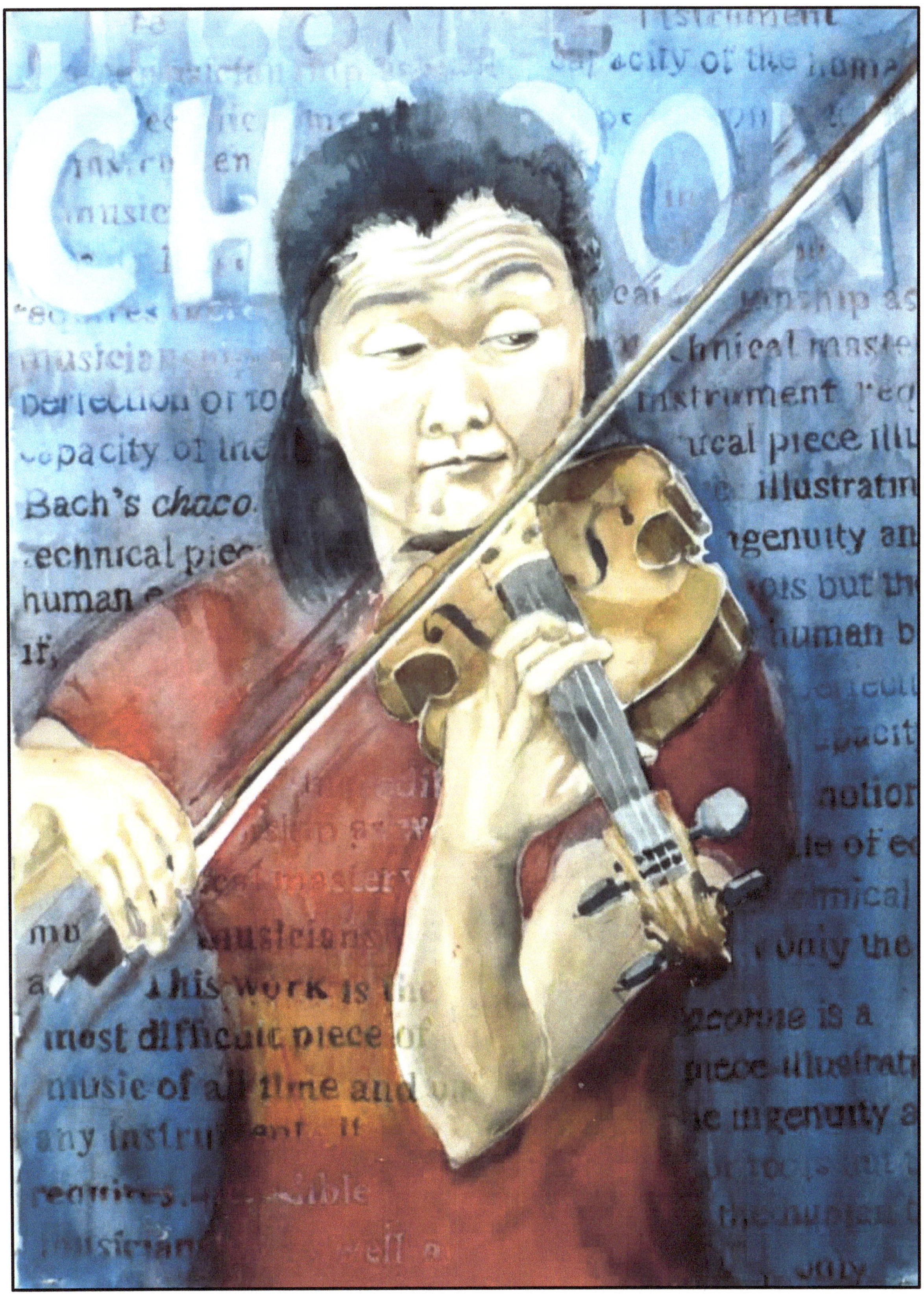

Figure 24. #773 Aiko. 2005 Watercolour and oil pencil on Arches Paper. 76x56cm

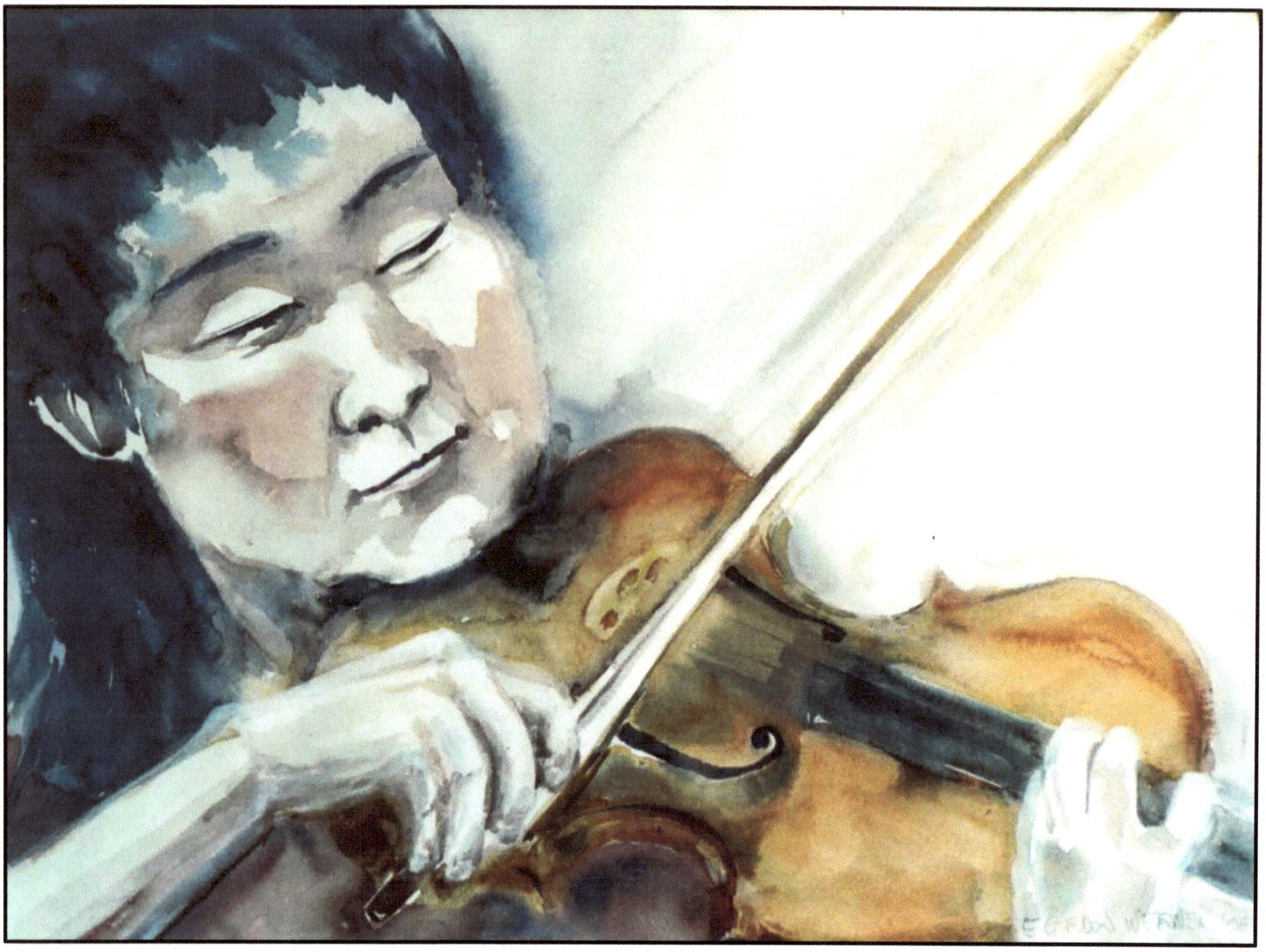

Figure 25. #774 Aiko II. 2005 Watercolour on Arches Paper. 76x56cm

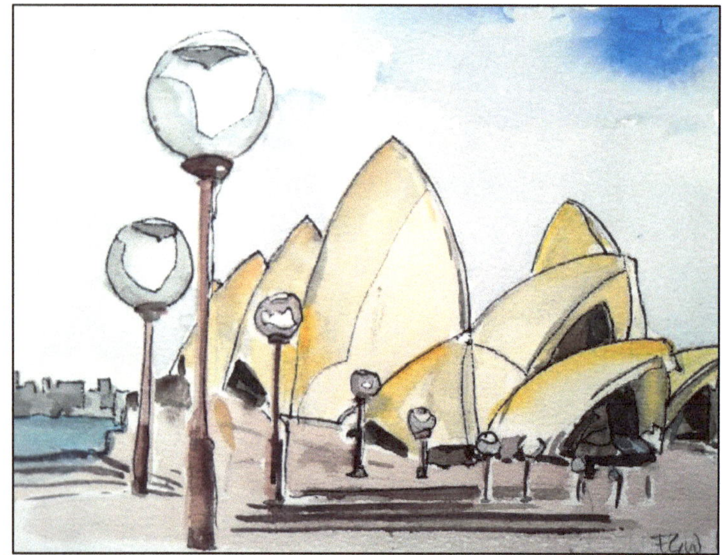

Figure 27. #1342 Sydney Opera House, near Aiko's practise venue

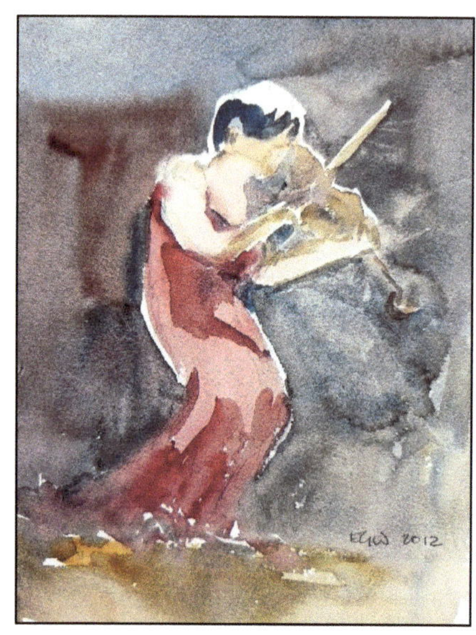

Figure 26 #2559 Aiko in concert

Richard Tognetti and the Maribor Music Festival

Richard Tognetti who is Artistic Director and Lead Violin of the Australian Chamber Orchestra directed the Maribor Music Festival for 6 years from 2008. In 2009 I asked if I could sketch during rehearsals and Richard consented. It was to be the first of several visits for me to this dynamic music festival in Maribor, Slovenia.

Concerts were held at 11am and 7:30 pm each day and often at 5pm as well, bringing together an array of internationally renowned musicians, many of whom stayed on after their solo performances and played with larger orchestral groups. It was musical immersion, and I spent the days sketching and listening.

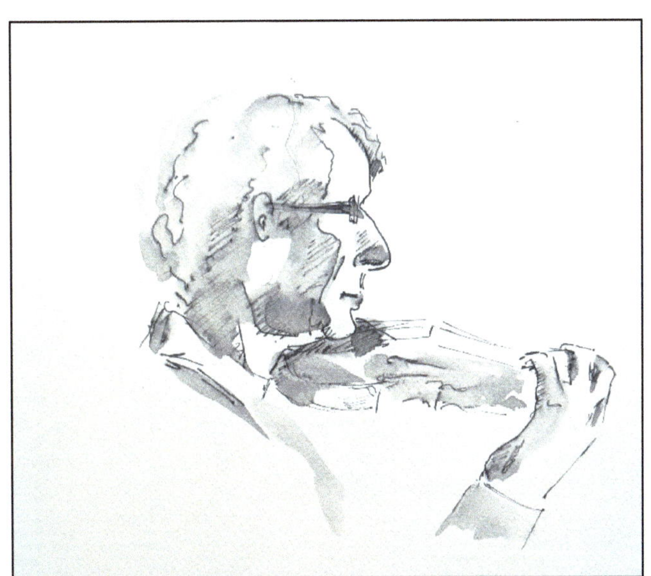

Figure 29. #1791.

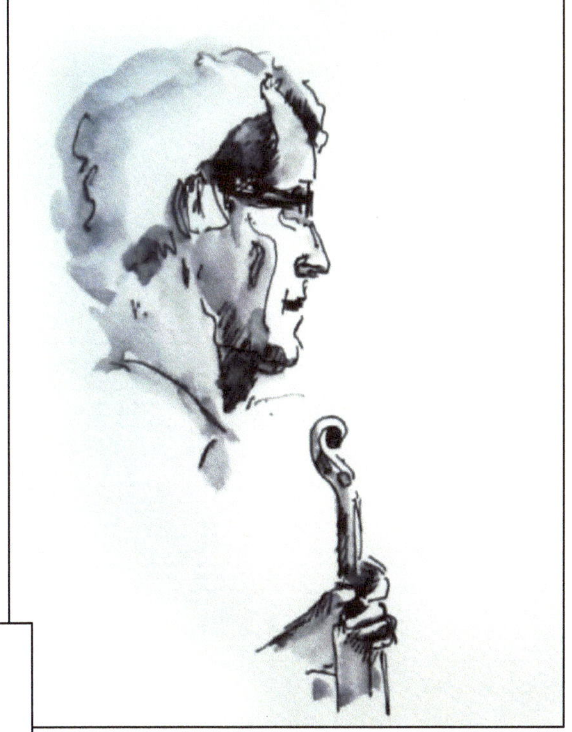

Figure 30. #1793.

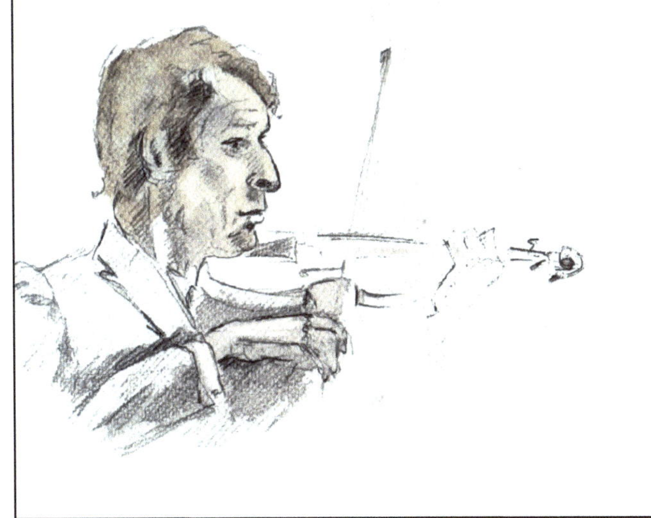

Figure 31. #1799.

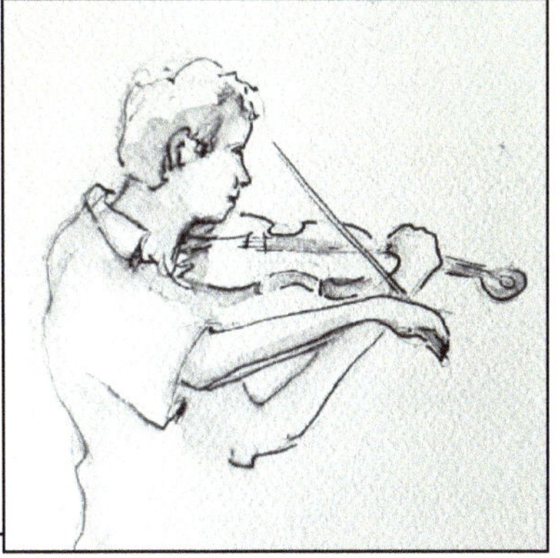

Figure 28. #1782.

Richard Tognetti Portraits

Back in my studio I painted portraits of Richard using the quick sketches made during Maribor rehearsals.

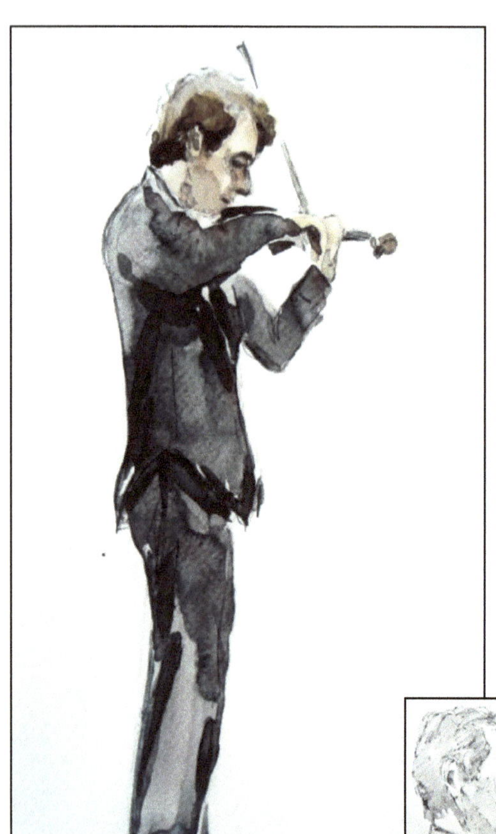

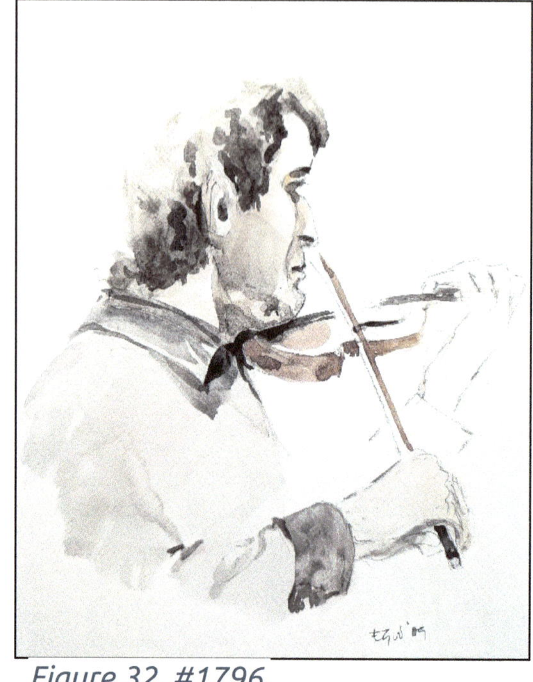

Figure 32. #1796.

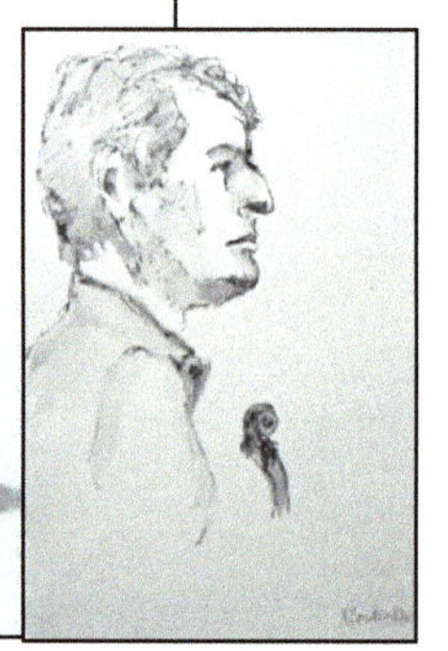

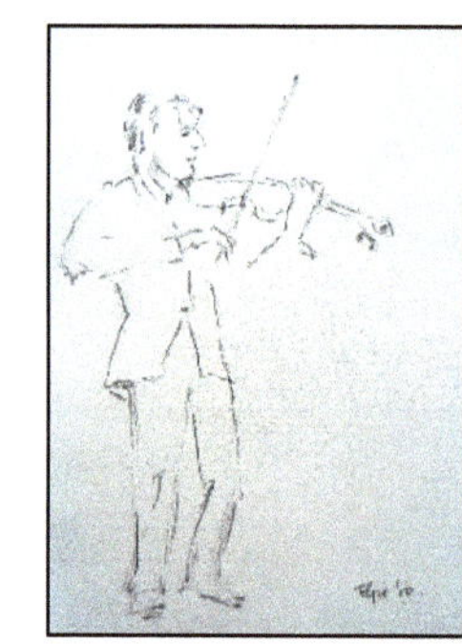

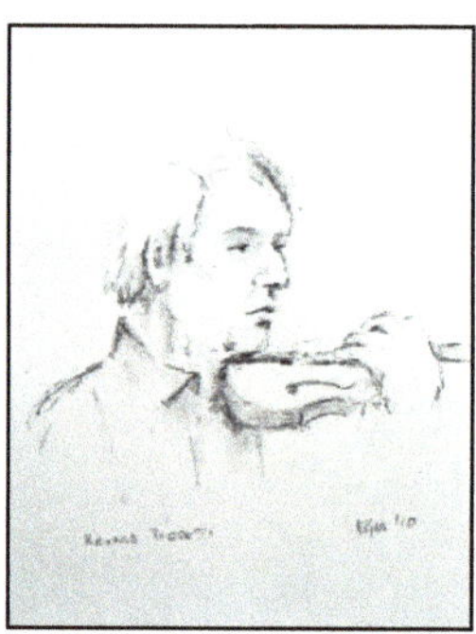

Figure 36 #1792

Figure 35. #1795

Figure 33. #2109

Figure 34. #2056

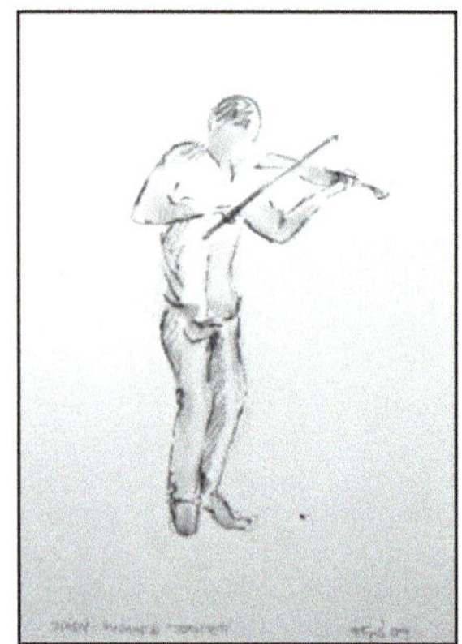

Figure 37. #1780

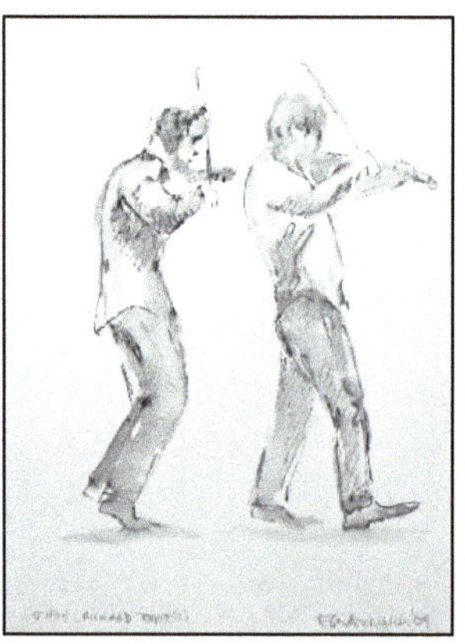

Figure 40 #1815

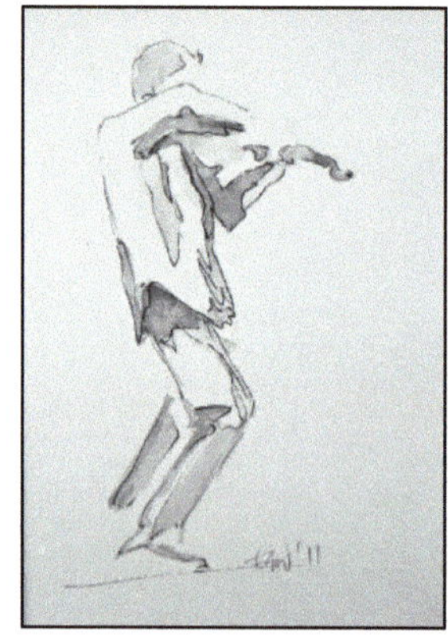

Figure 39 #2298

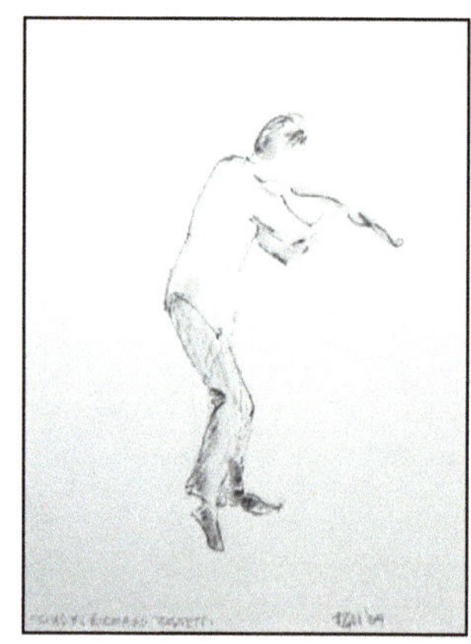

Figure 38 #1779

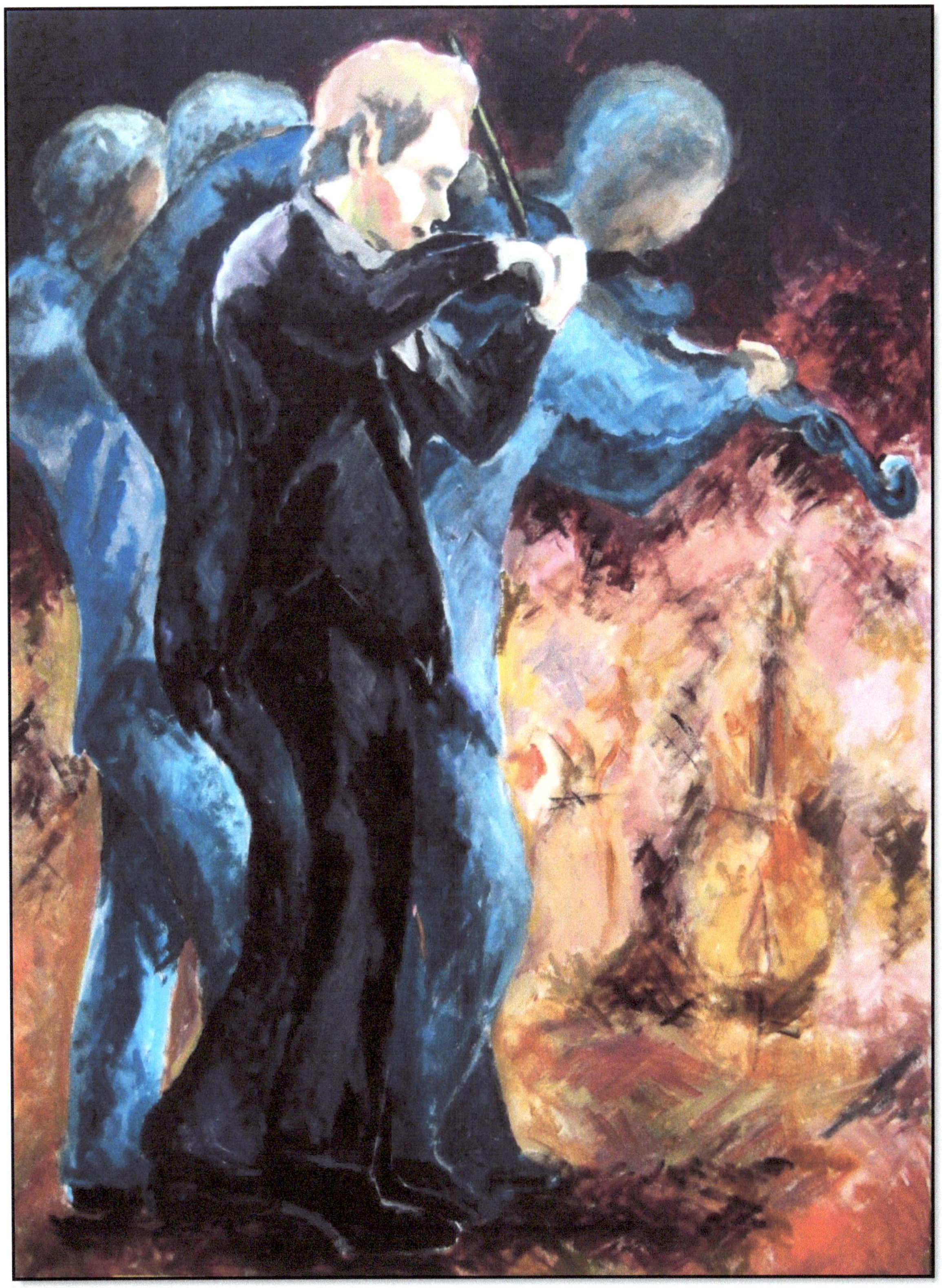

Figure 41. #1872 Tognetti in Action. 2009 Acrylic on Canvas. 101x76cm

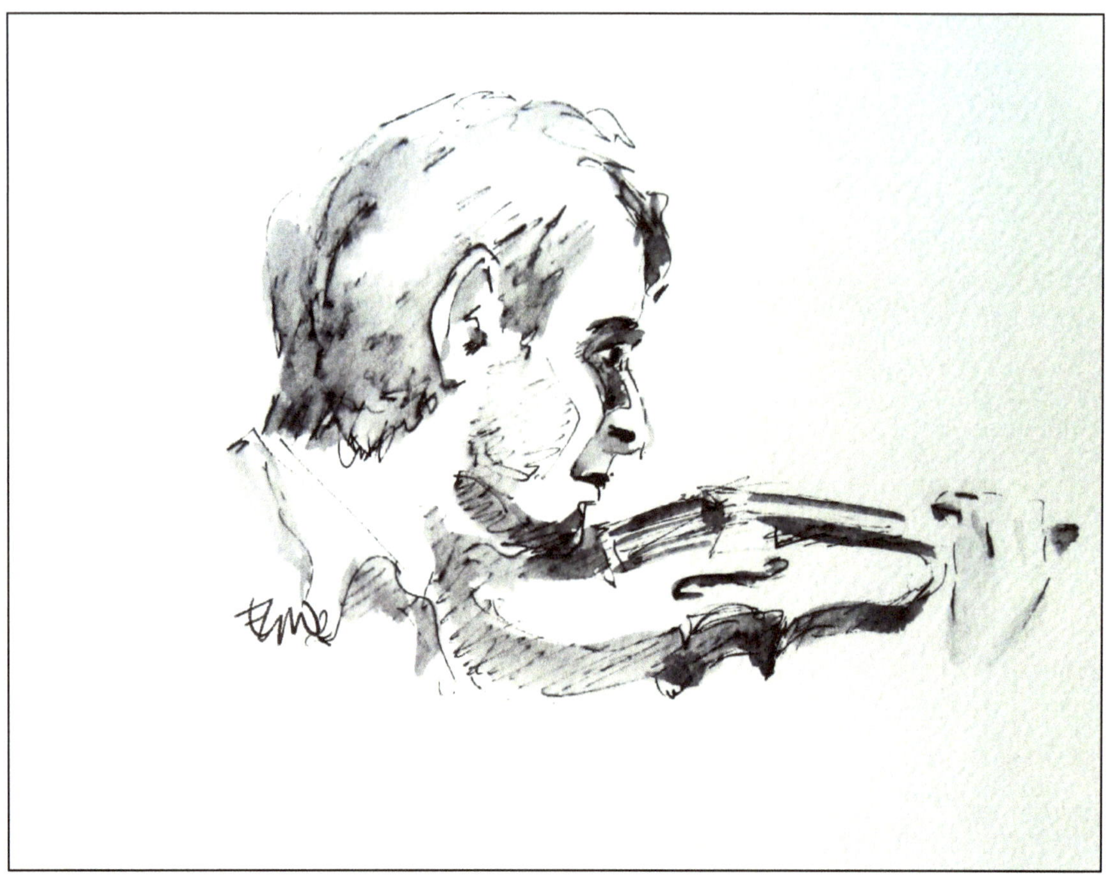

Figure 42. #1794 Ink sketch, Maribor Music Festival 2009.

I had visited the Nolde Museum in Berlin after the Maribor Music Festival and the small colourful 'forbidden' works by Emil Nolde inspired my second Tognetti portrait, *#1871 Pink Violin*. I was aiming to paint the intense concentration of the violinist, captured in sketch #1794. This portrait was submitted to the Archibald Prize in 2010.

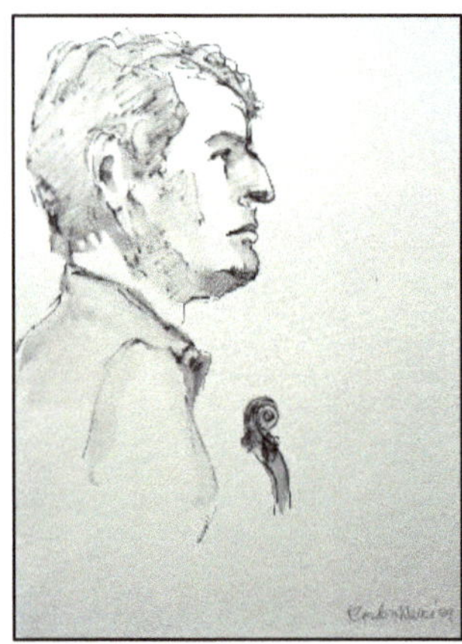

Figure 43. #1795

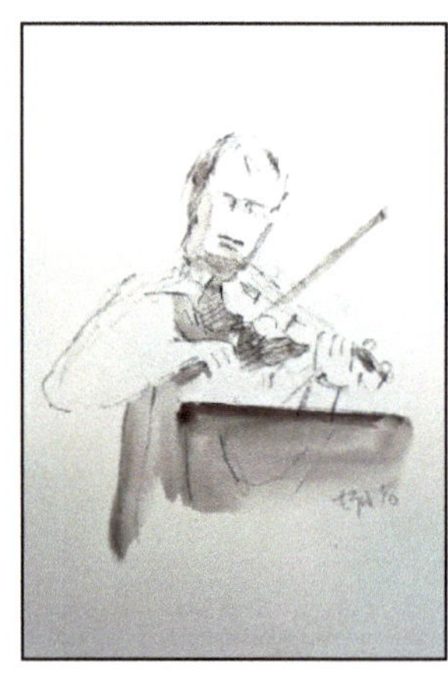

Figure 44 #2088

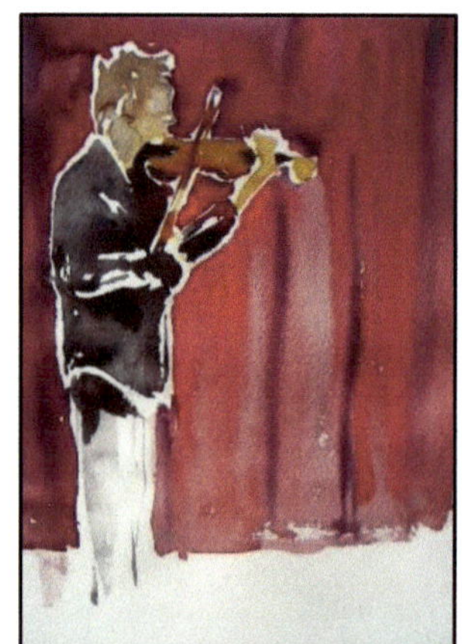

Figure 45. #2329

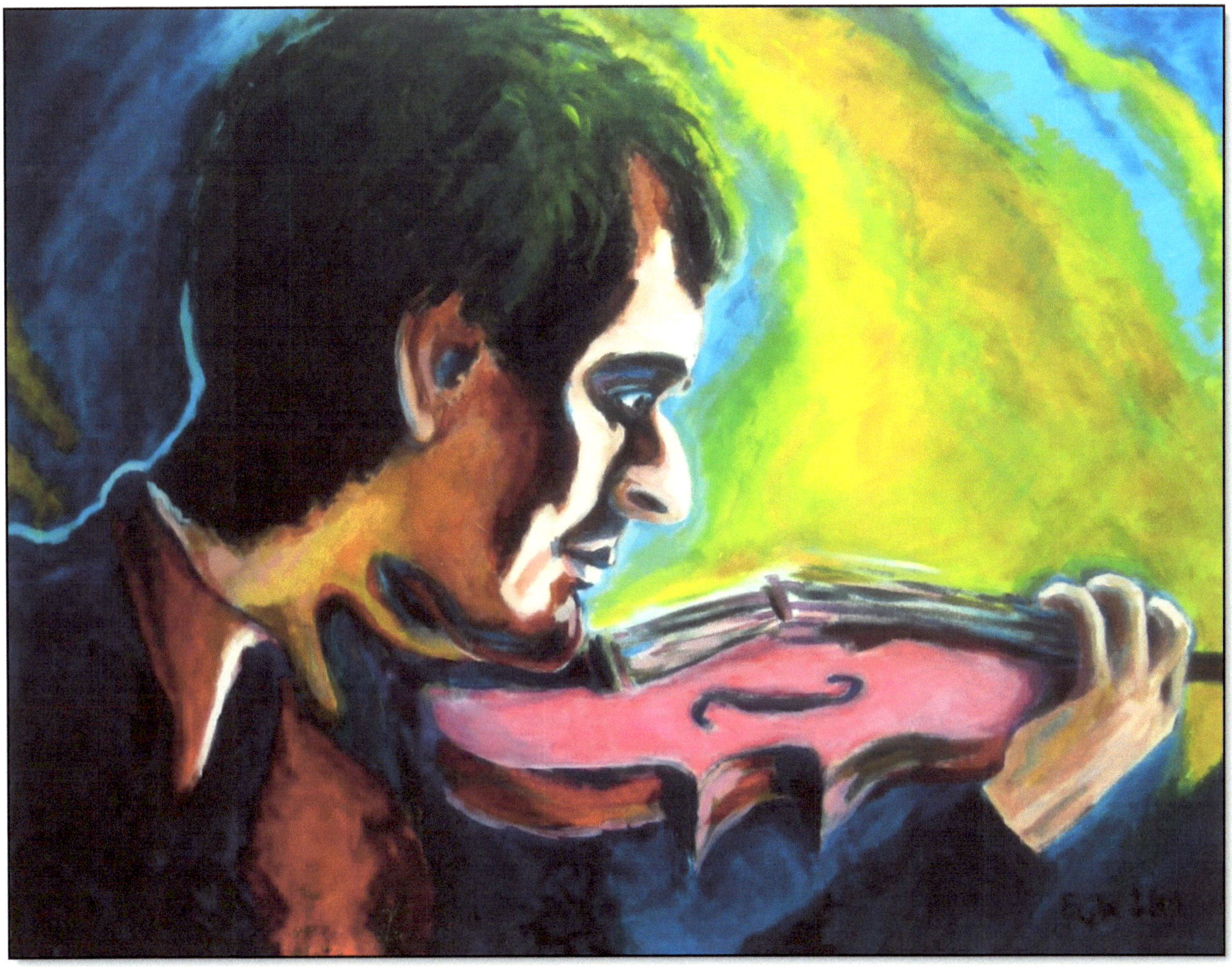

Figure 46 #1871 Pink Violin: Richard Tognetti in Maribor. 2009. Acrylic on Canvas 101x96cm

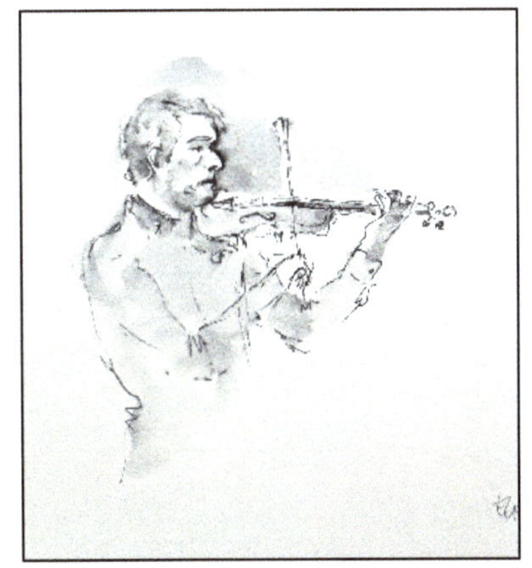

Figure 49. #1798

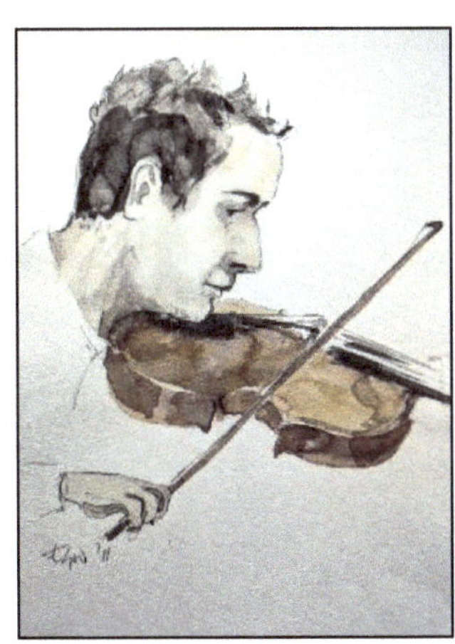

Figure 48. #2320

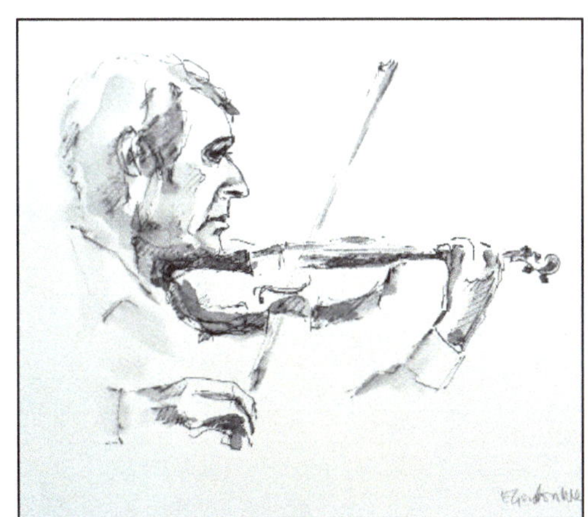

Figure 47. #1800

Violinist in Blue

Sketches of Richard Tognetti used for the painting #2226 *Violinist on Blue.*

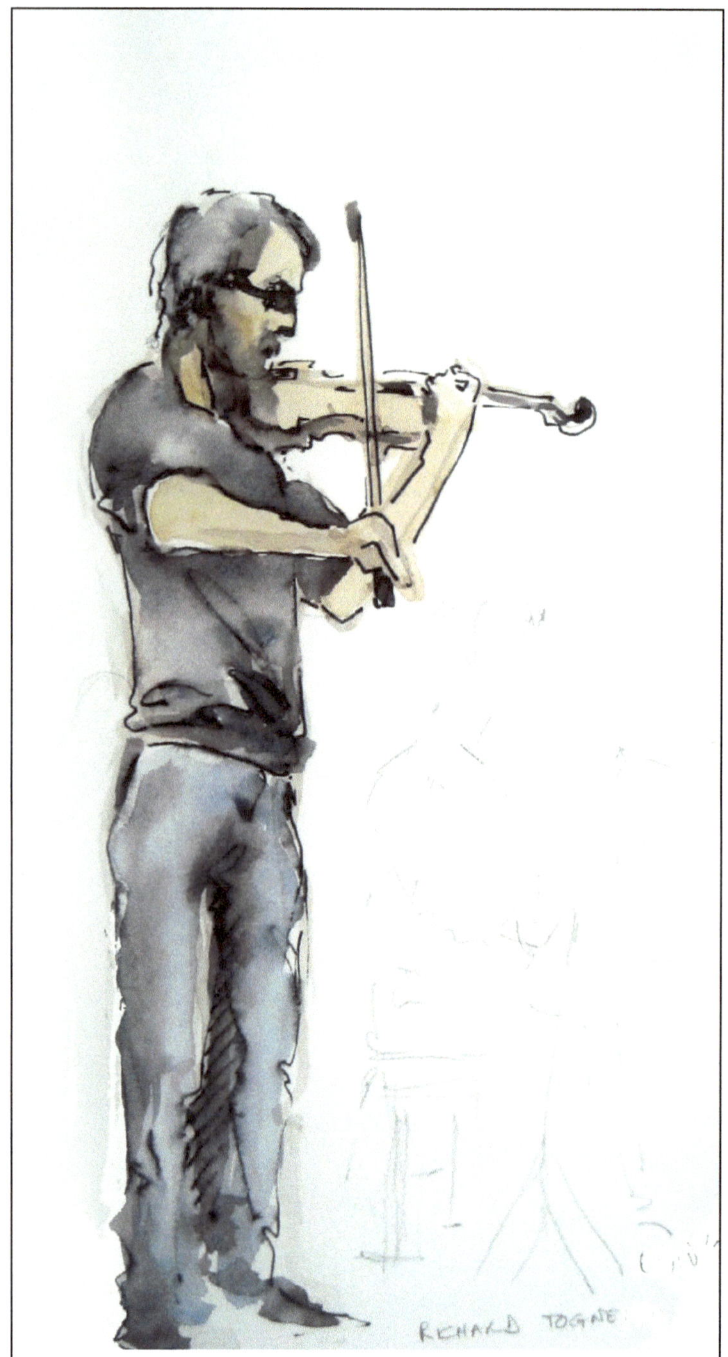

Figure 52 #2063 Richard Tognetti.

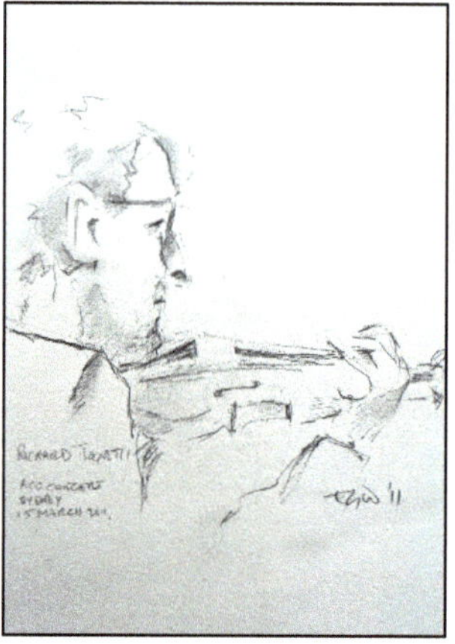

Figure 53. #2268

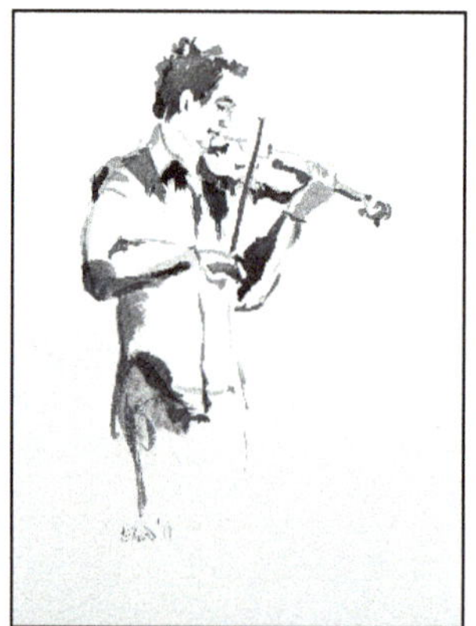

Figure 51. #2326

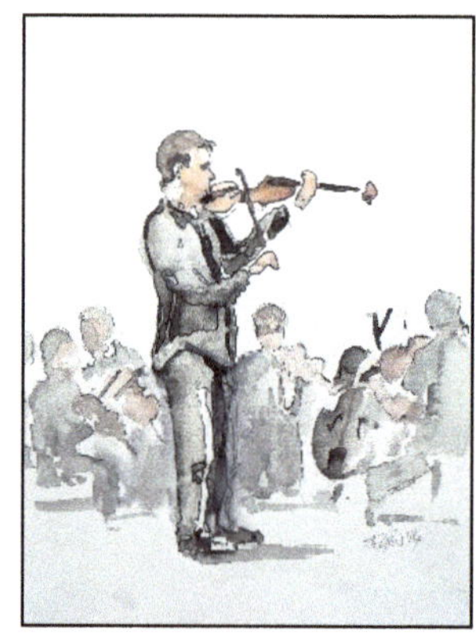

Figure 50. #2781

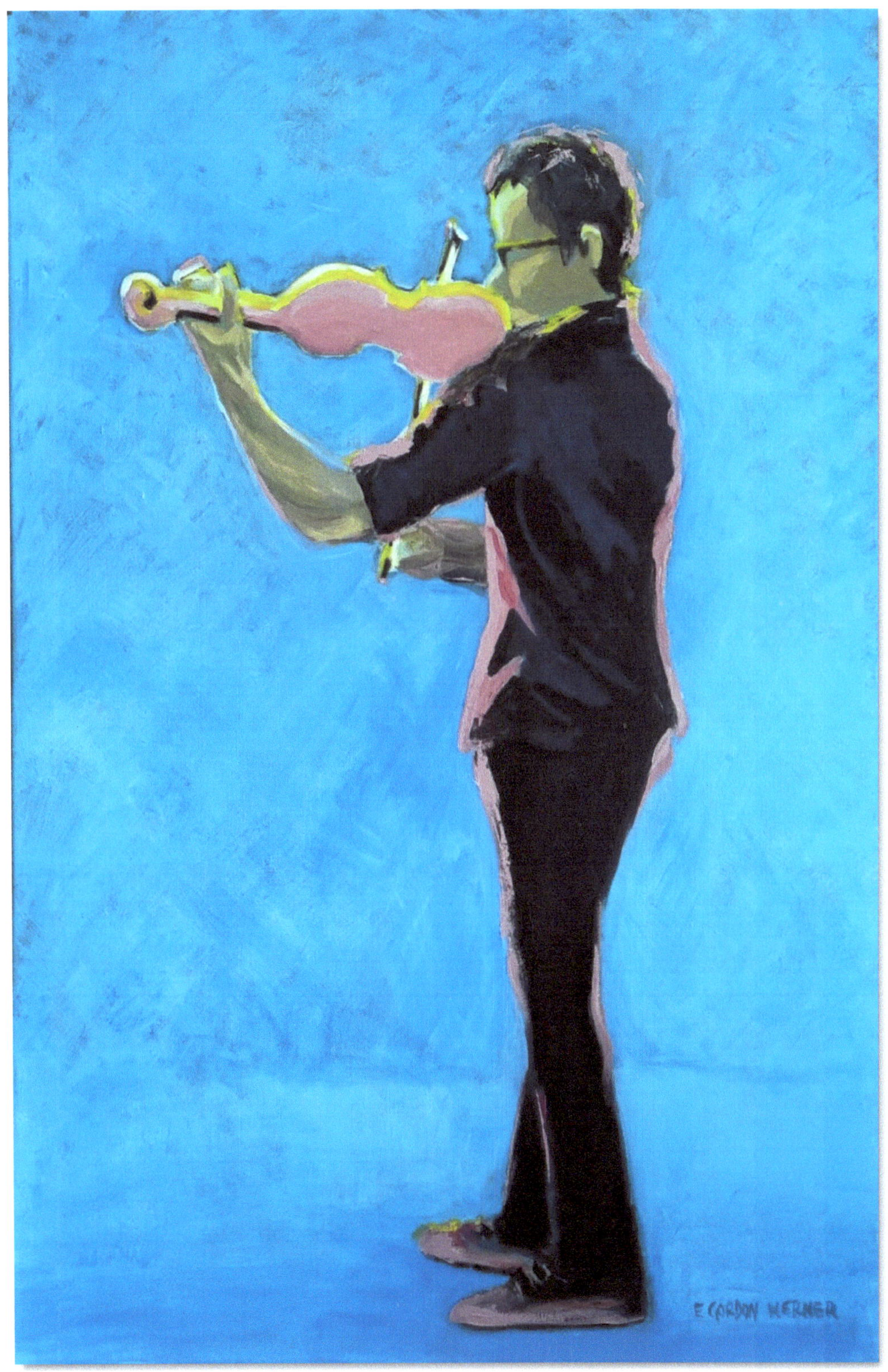

Figure 54 #2226 Violinist on Blue. 2010 90 x 60 cm. Oil on Canvas

Australian Chamber Orchestra in Maribor

Maribor was the 2012 EU City of Culture, and the Australian Chamber Orchestra were in Maribor for the duration of the Maribor Music Festival. They came direct from London where they had performed to rave reviews and repeated their performance in Maribor to an equally warm reception from the packed concert hall.

I took the opportunity and made watercolour sketches of as many orchestra members as I could in preparation for later portraits.

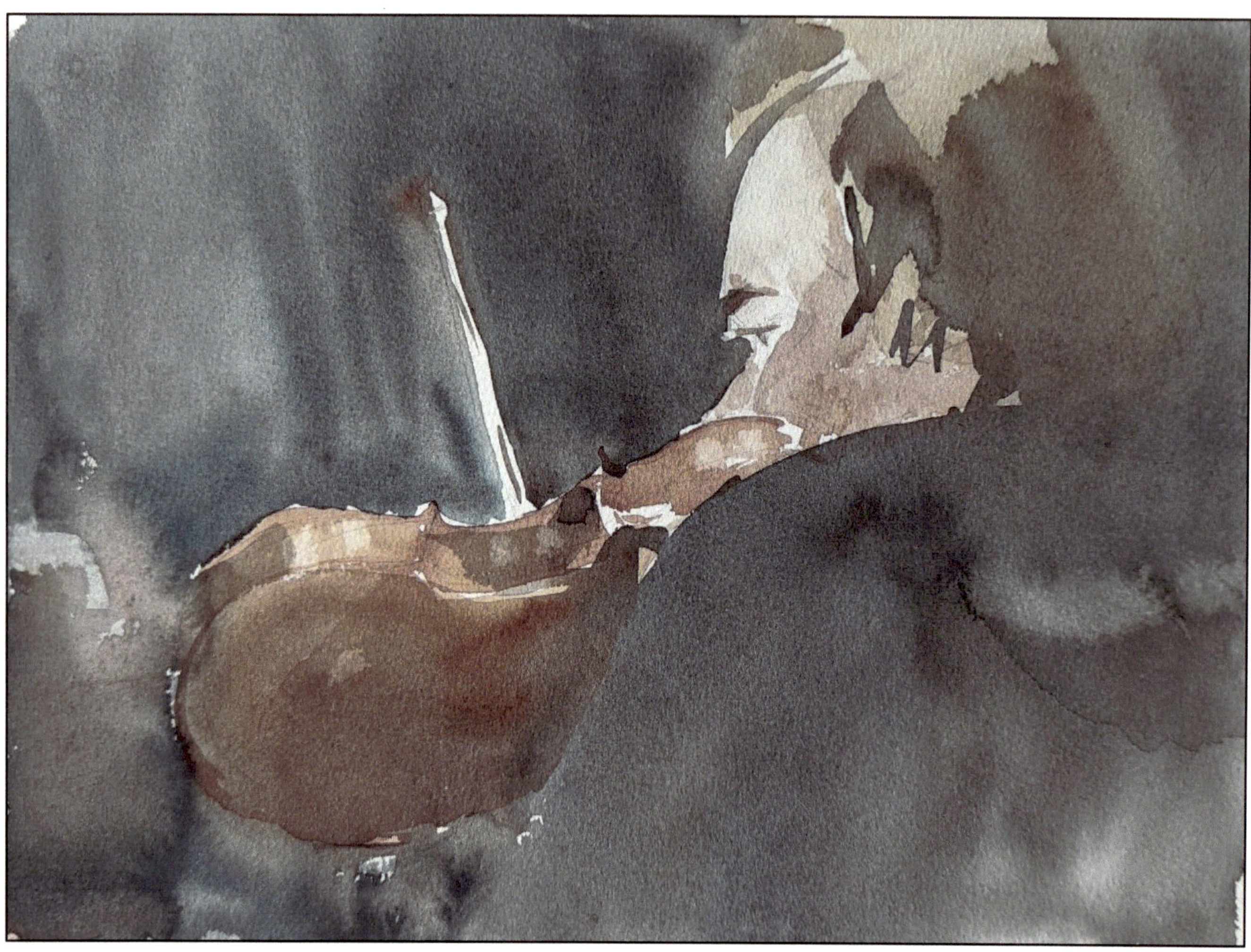

Figure 55 #2591 Richard Tognetti with violin

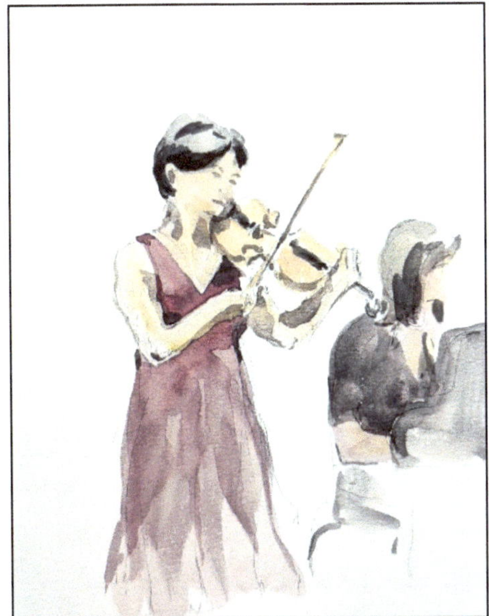

Figure 56 #2591 Aiko Goto

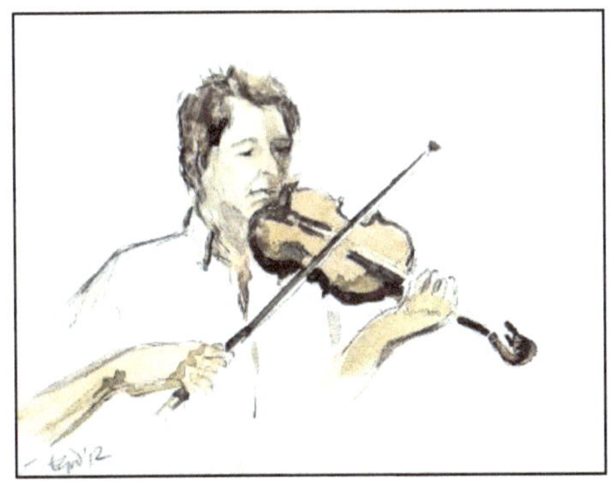

Figure 59 #2542 Richard Tognetti

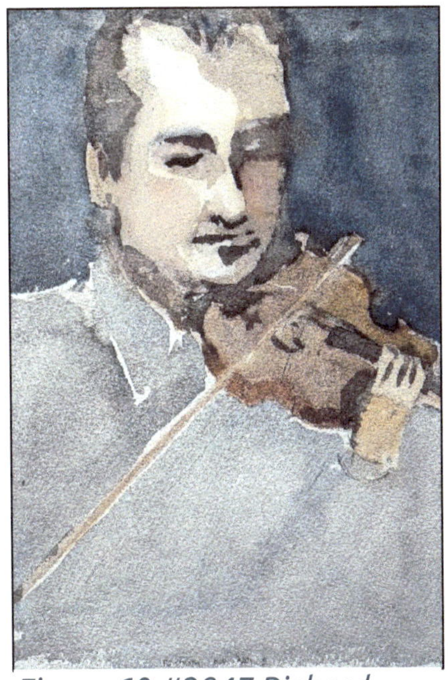

Figure 60 #2847 Richard Tognetti

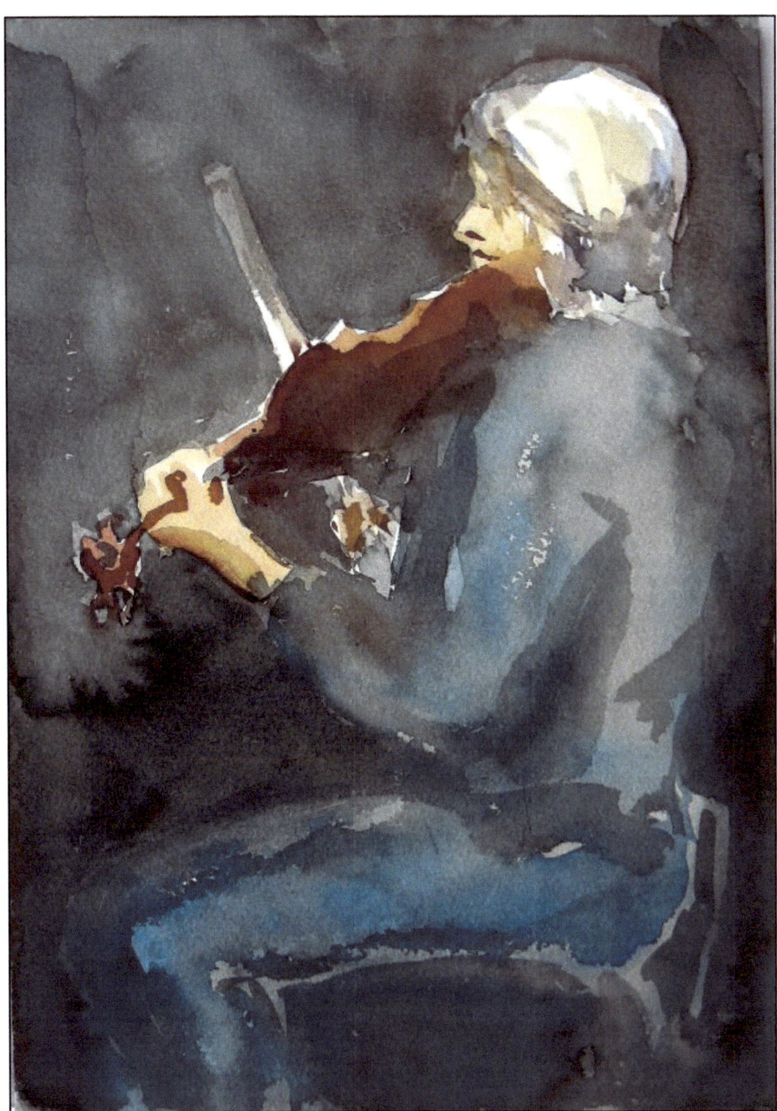

Figure 58 #2597 Helena Rathbone

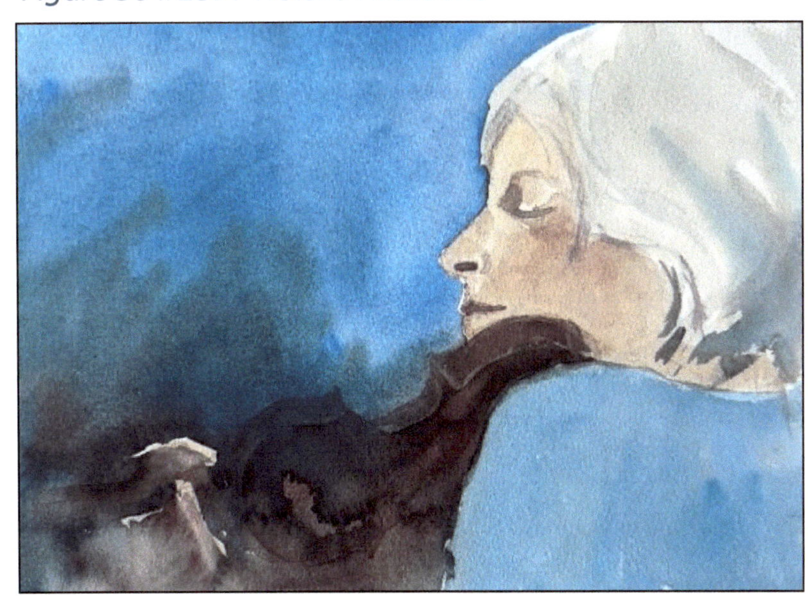

Figure 57. #2564 Helene Rathbone

Satu Vänskä, Violin

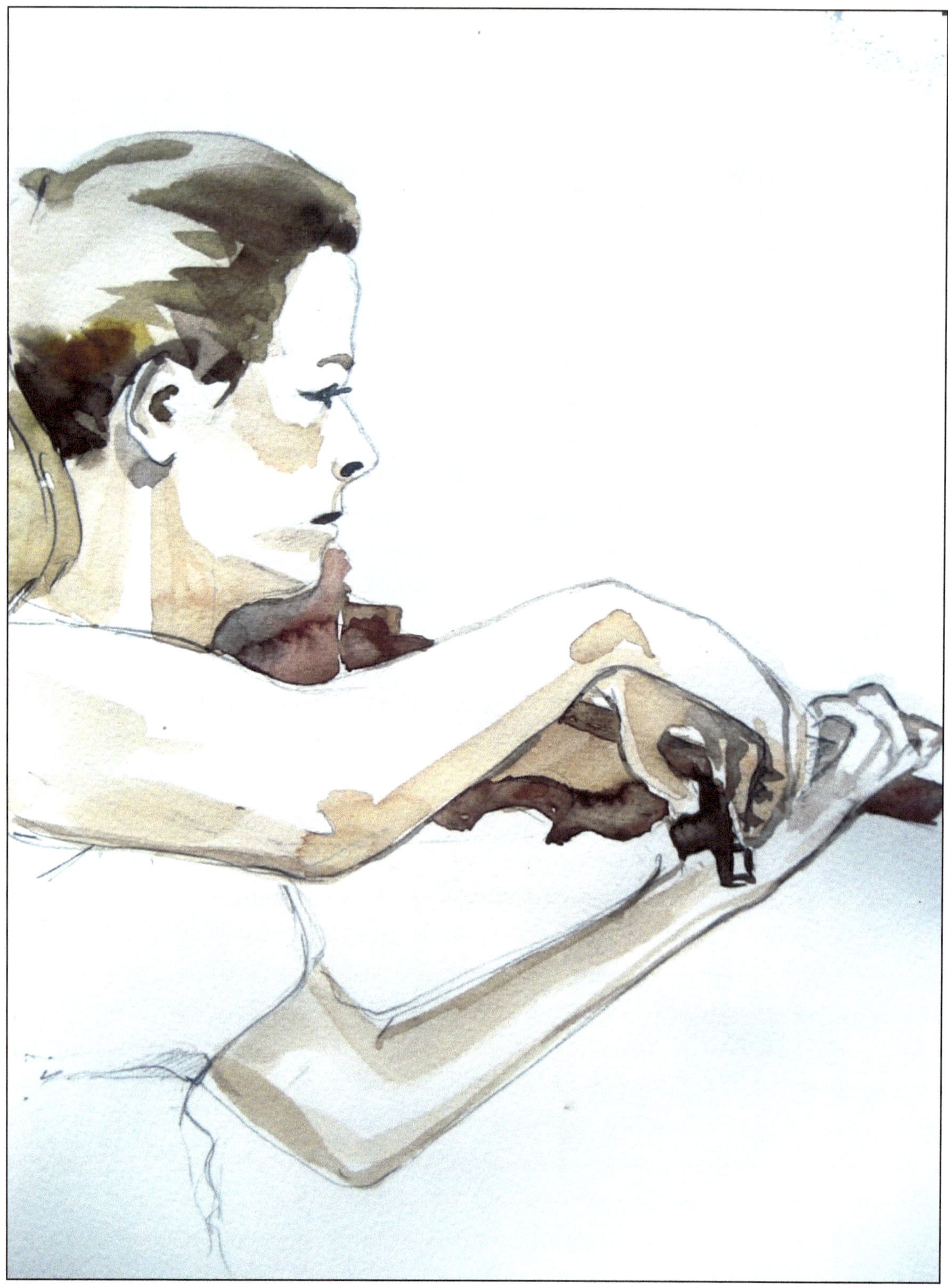

Figure 61 #2544 Satu Vänskä, Principal Violin.

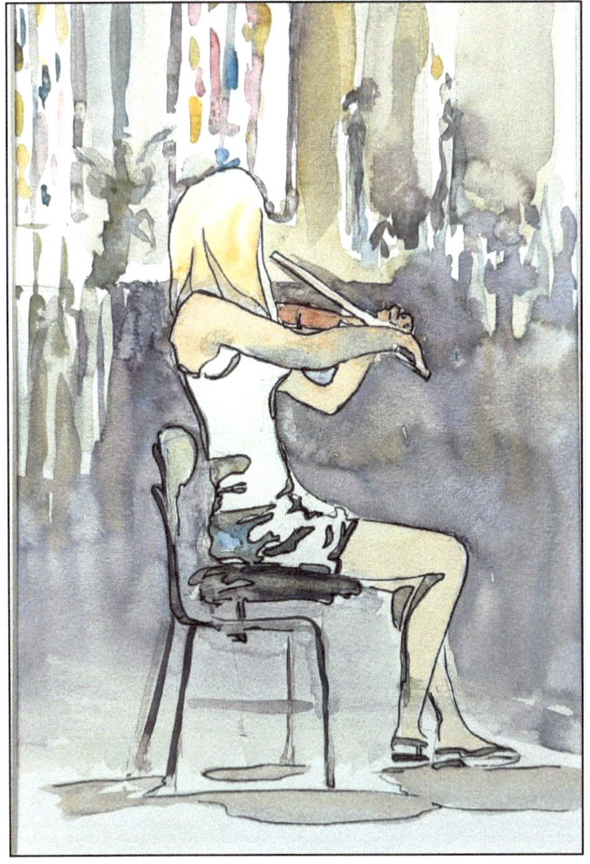

Figure 63. #2340

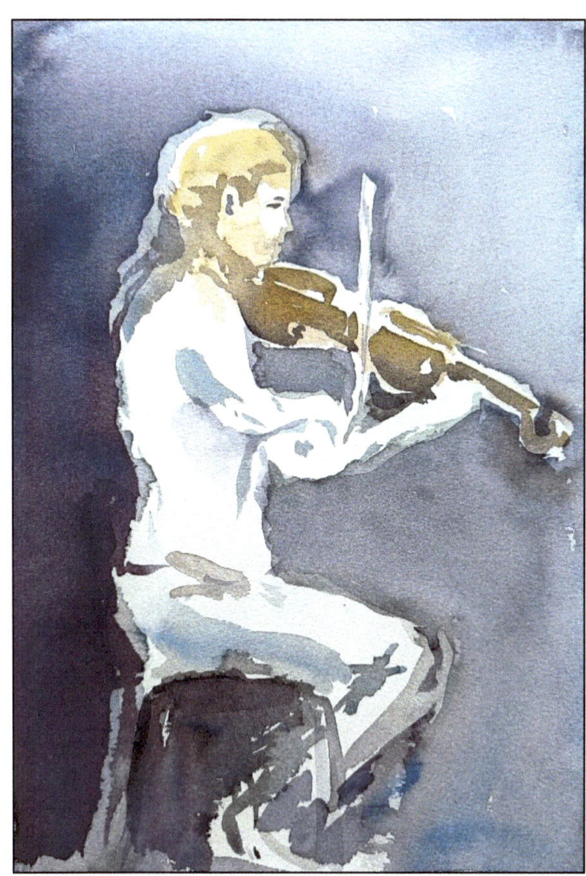

Figure 62 #2593

In 2012 ACO Principal Violin Satu Vänskä sang at a Maribor concert. Satu is not only a virtuoso violinist but has a lovely voice and good comic timing. She was often at the front of the stage in Maribor and I wanted to paint her for an entry to the Archibald Portrait Prize, so I drew her as often as I could.

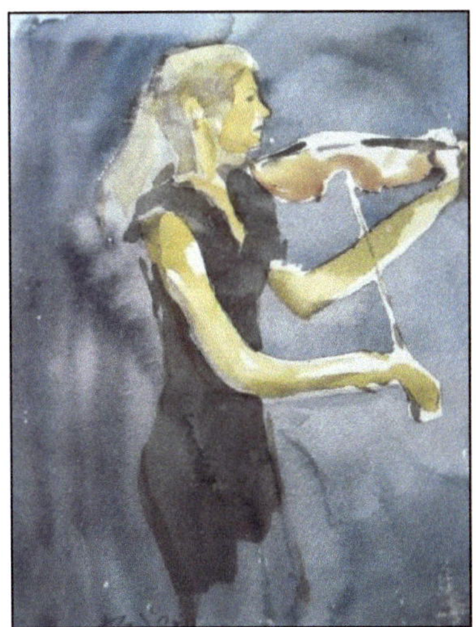

Figure 66 #U.

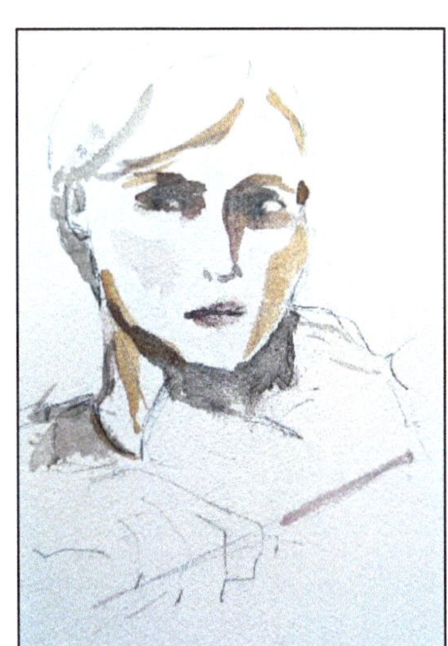

Figure 64 #U

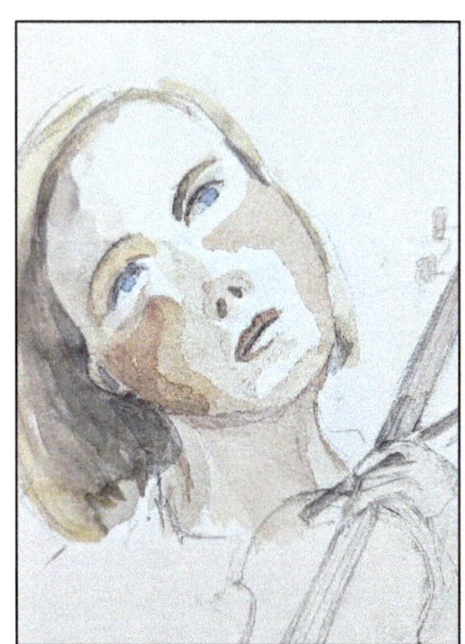

Figure 65. #1814

Christopher Moore, Viola

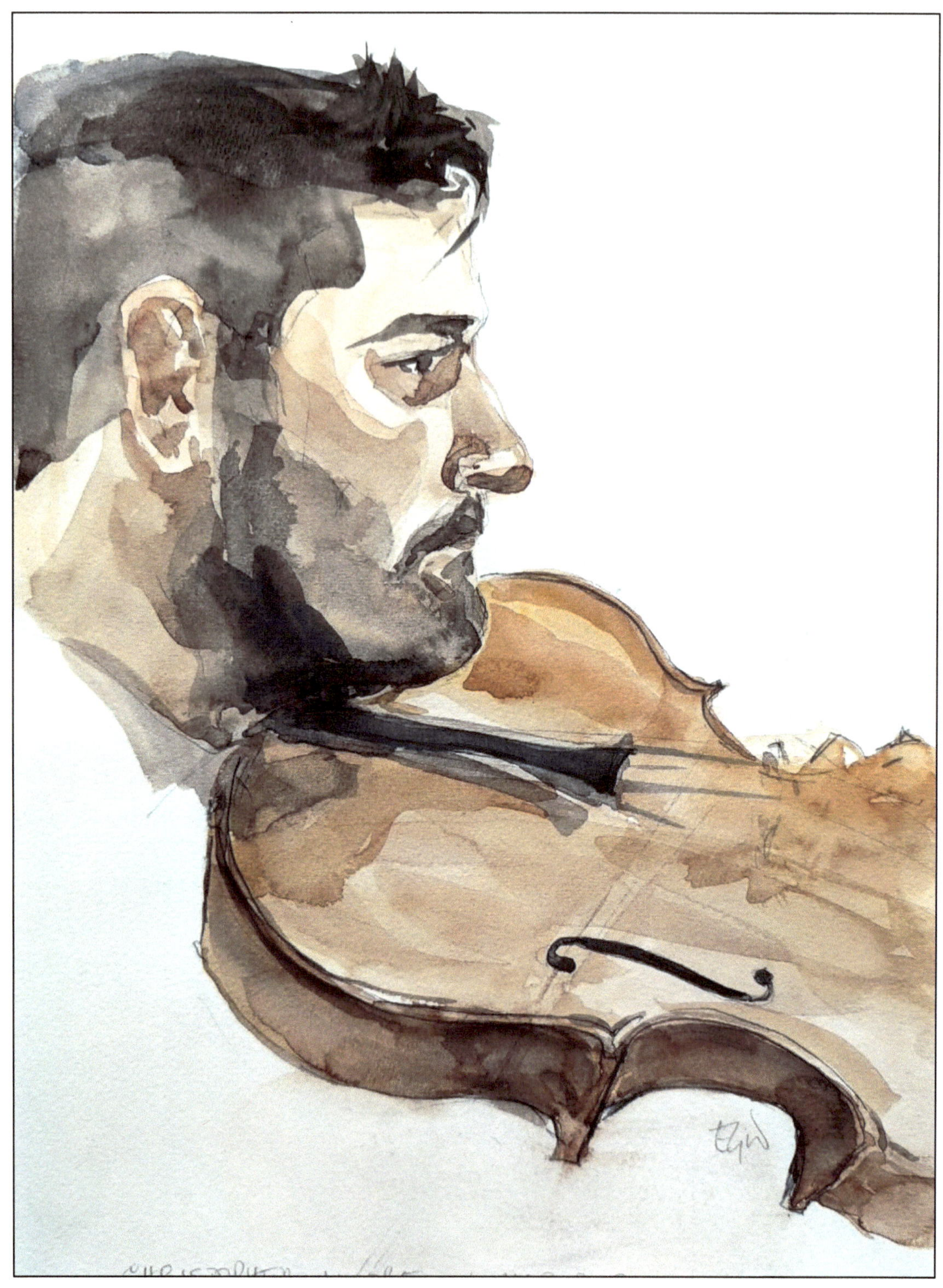

Figure 67. #2551 Christopher Moore, viola

Christopher Moore is now Principal Viola with the Melbourne Symphony Orchestra after nine years with the ACO. I hung my sketches of the musicians and of Maribor in the lobby of my hotel and sketch #2551 of Christopher attracted a lot of attention from concert goers.

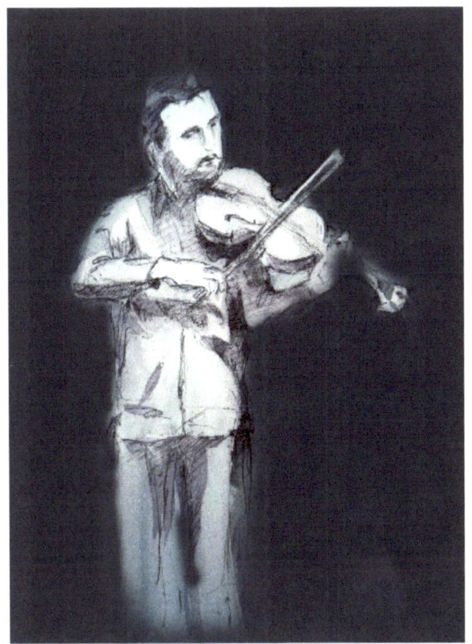

Figure 69 #2091

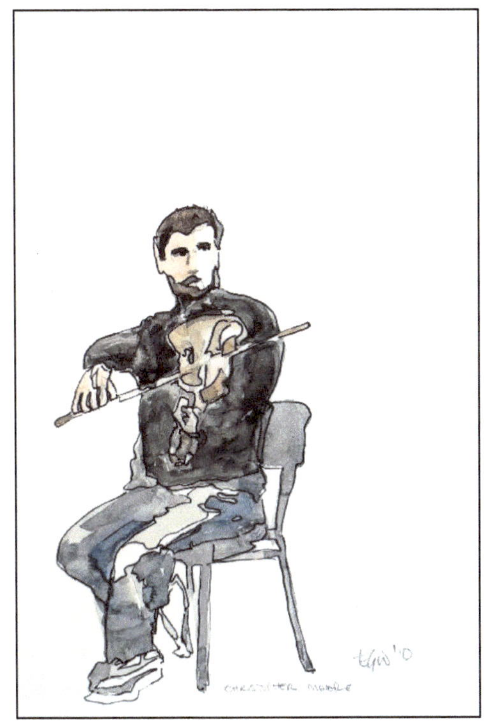

Figure 68 #2054

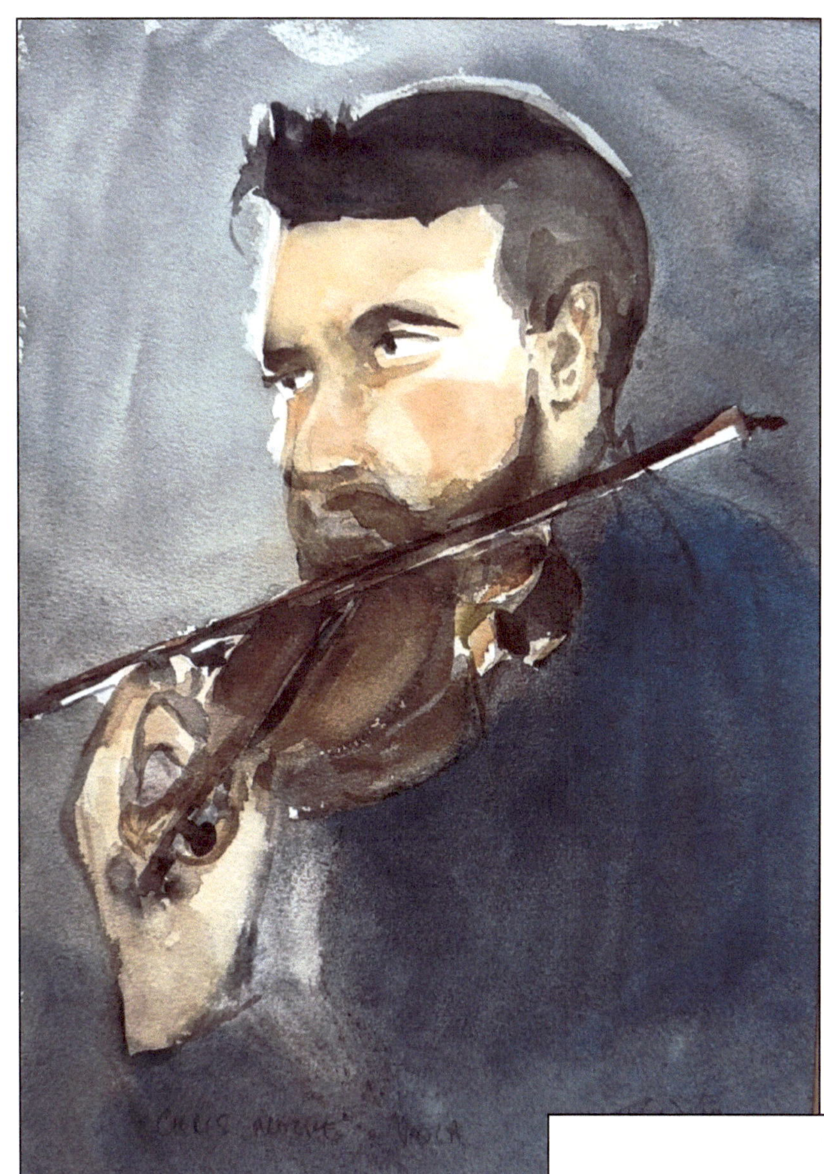

Figure 71. 2549, Christopher Moore, Viola

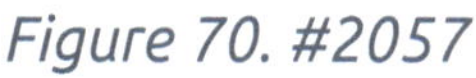

Figure 70. #2057

Timo-Veikko Valve

The cello is a favourite musical instrument for many as are the ACO cellists Timo-Veikko Valve, Melissa Barnard and Julian Thompson.

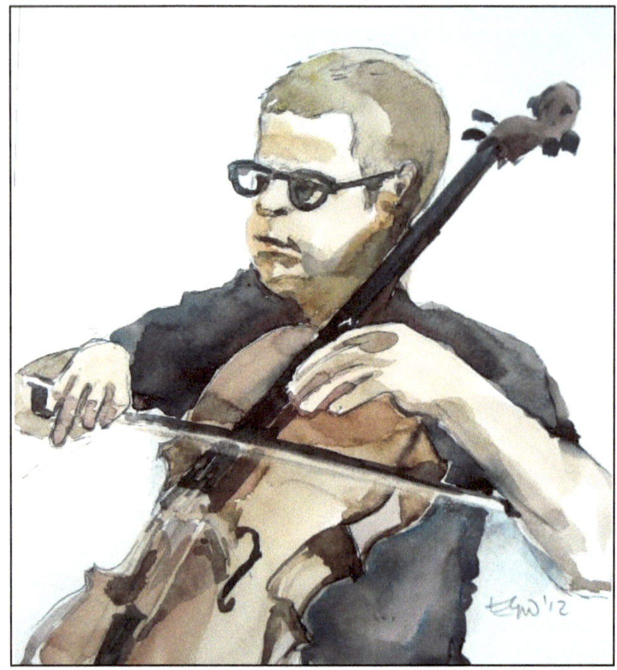

Figure 73. 2543 Timo Veikko Valve

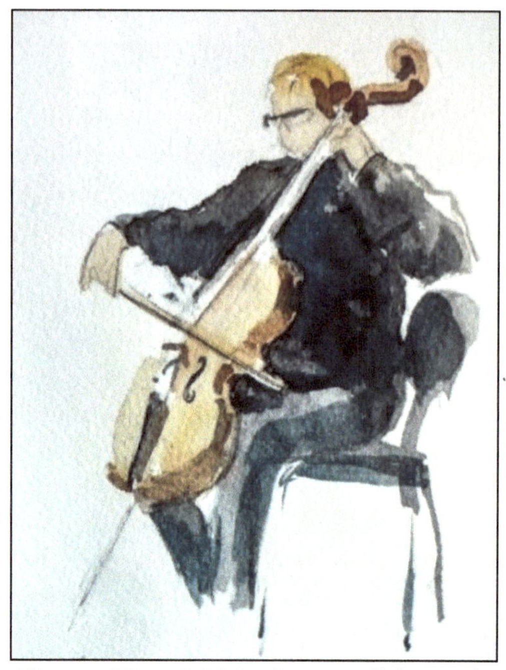

Figure 75. #2923 Timo-Veikko Valve

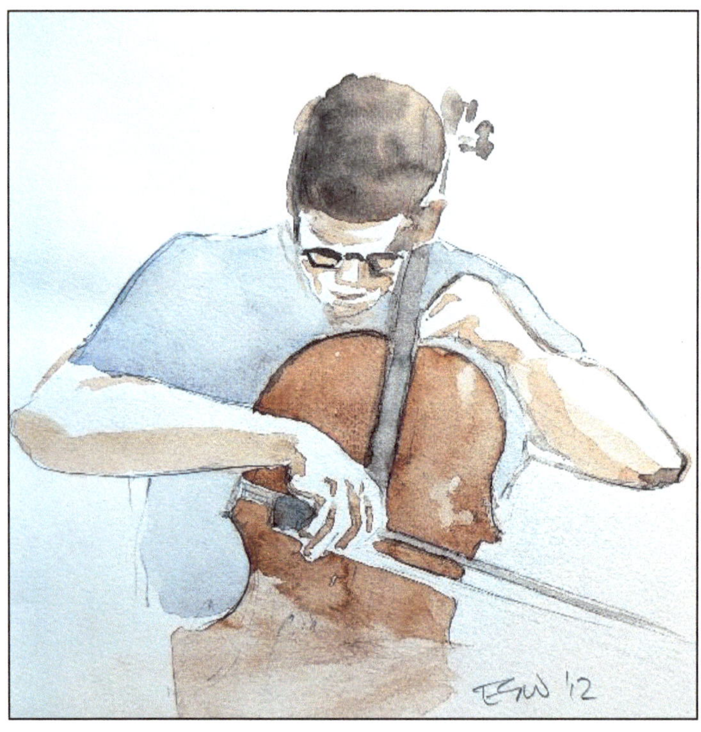

Figure 72 #2557 Timo-Veikko Valve

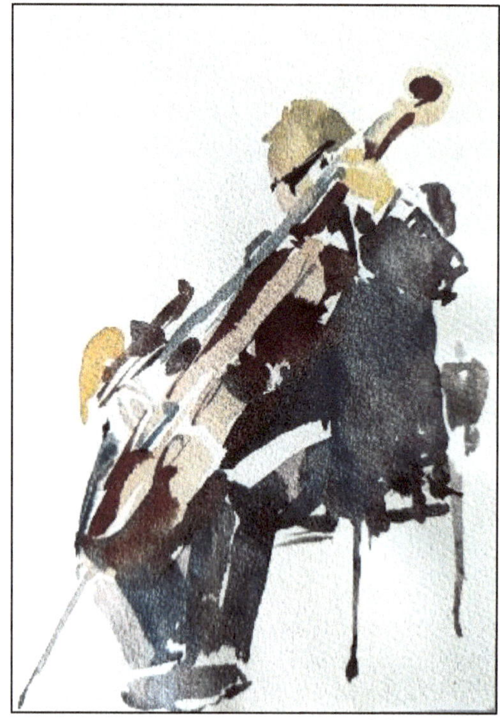

Figure 74 #2071 Timo Veikko Valve

Melissa Barnard and Julian Thompson

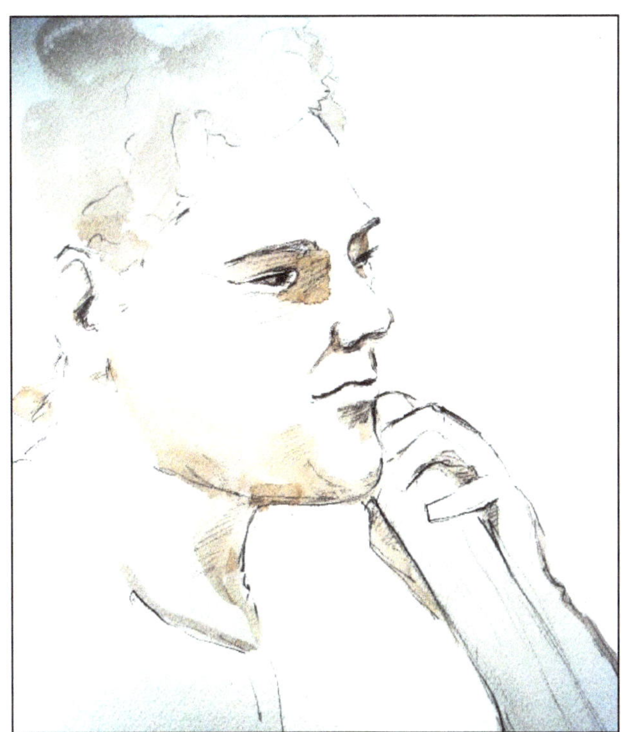

Figure 77. # 2566 Julian Thompson

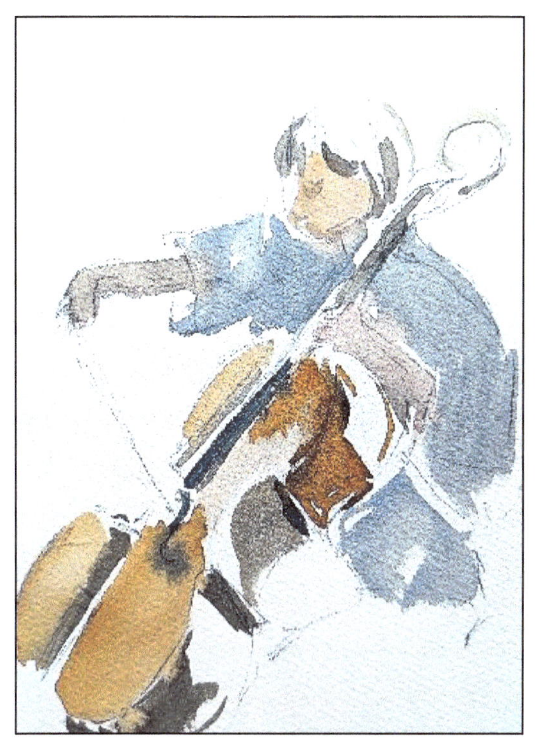

Figure 76 #928 Melissa

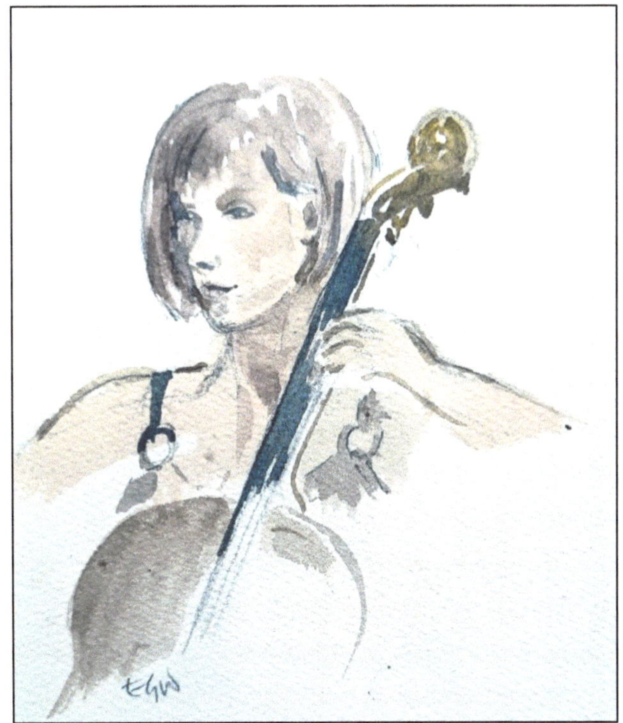

Figure 79 #926 Melissa Barnard

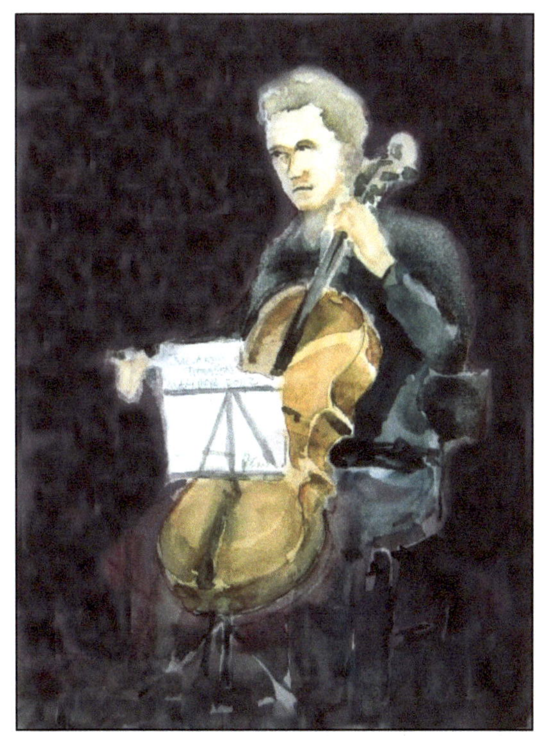

Figure 78. #2545 Julian Thompson

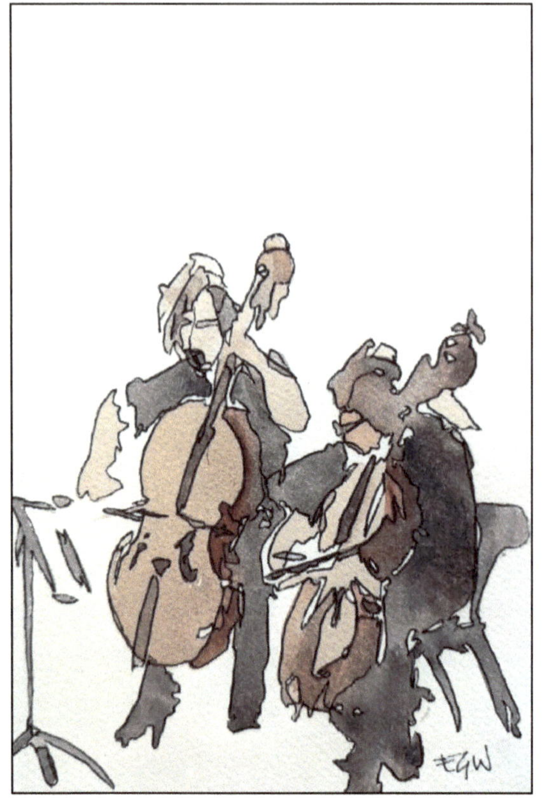

Figure 82 #1972 Melissa Barnard, Timo-Veikko Valve

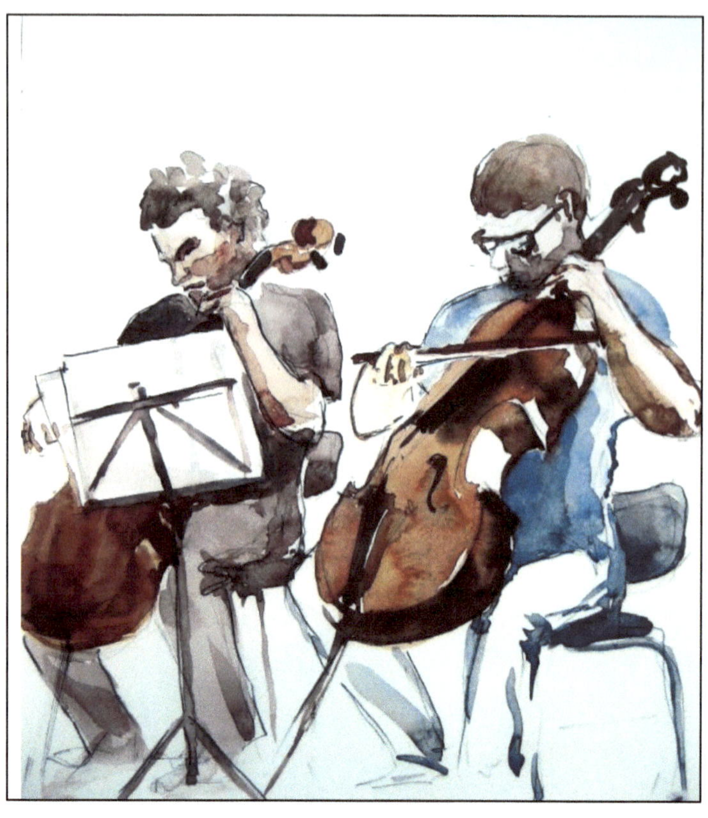

Figure 83 #2558 Julian Thompson and Timo-Veikko Valve

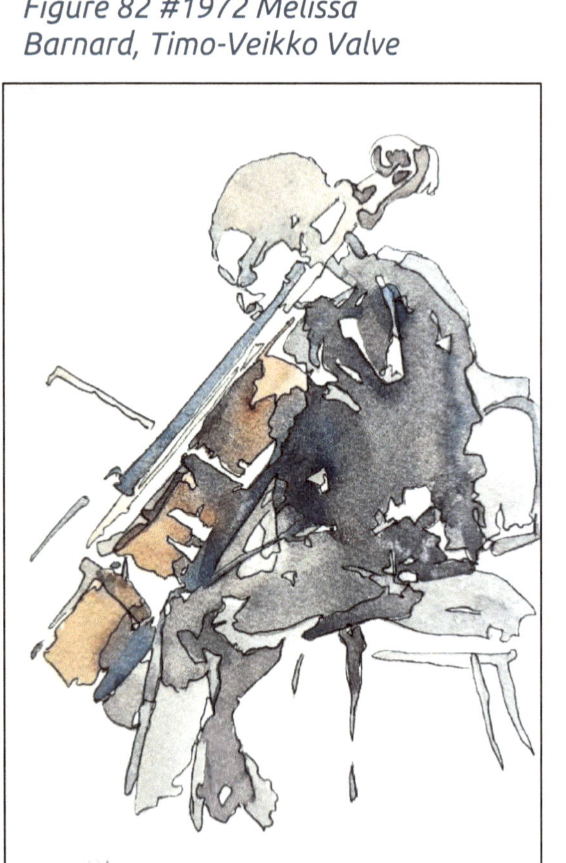

Figure 81. 2070 Timo-Veikko Valve

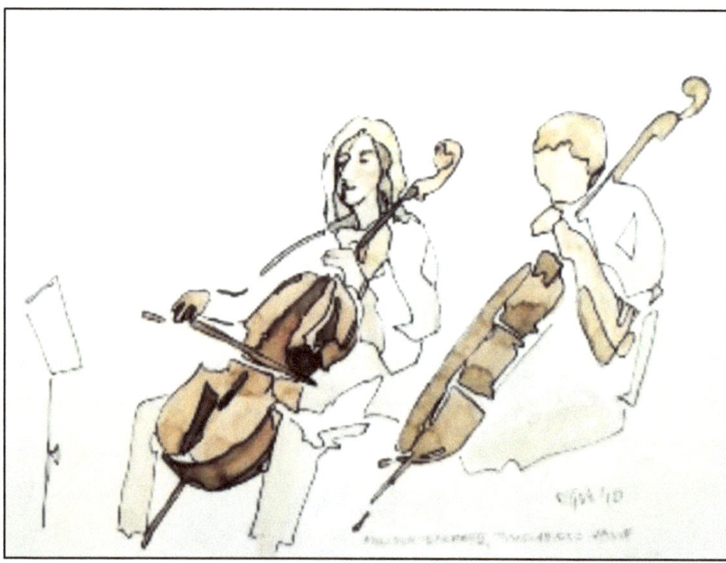

Figure 80. #2055 Melissa Barnard and Timo-Veikko Valve in 2010.

Maxime Bibeau

In 2012 Max Bibeau played a huge Double Bass made in the 16th century. It has the most mellow sound and is bigger than most double basses. This bass shines from within.

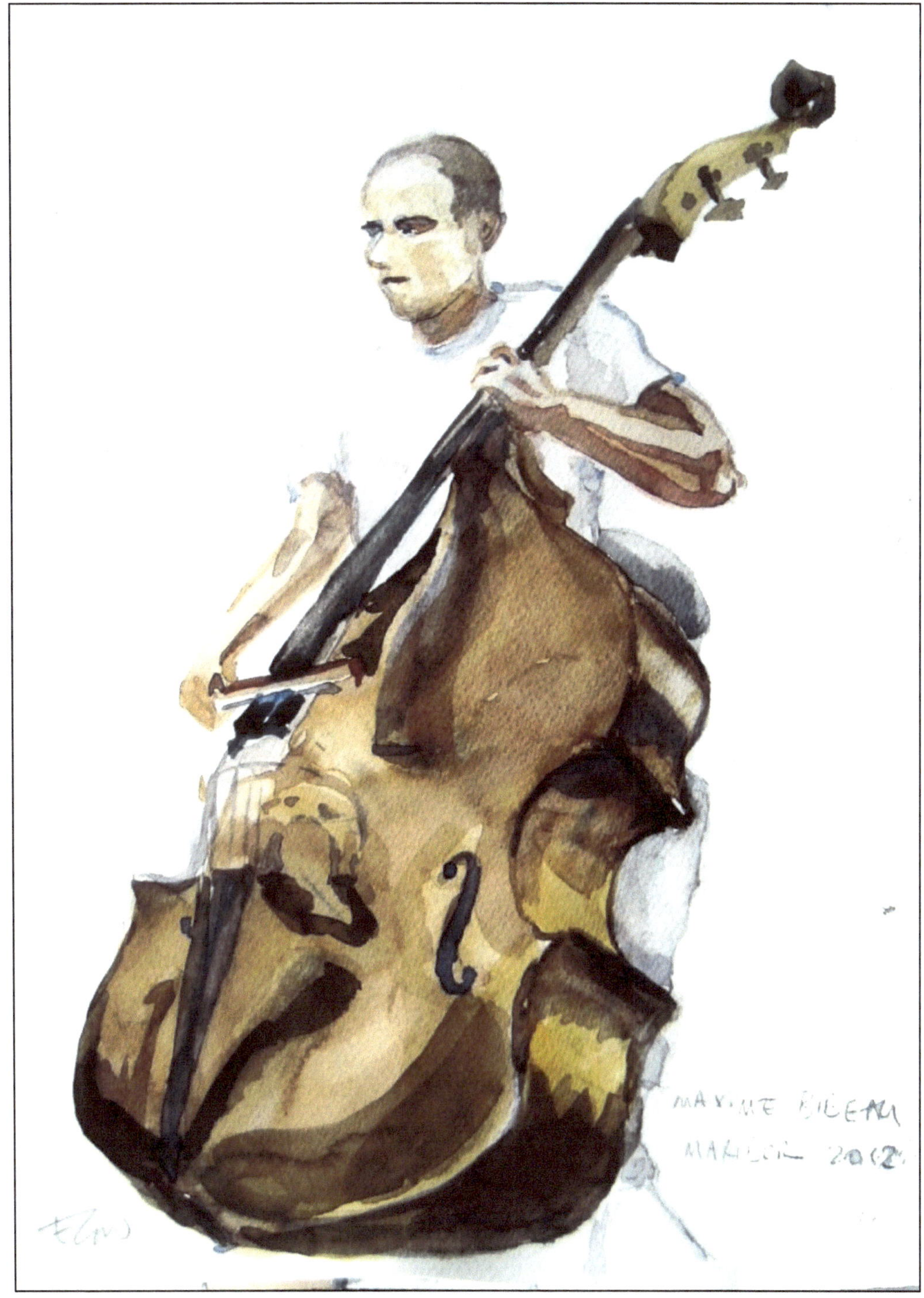

Figure 84. #2546 Maxime Bibeau with 16th Century Double Bass

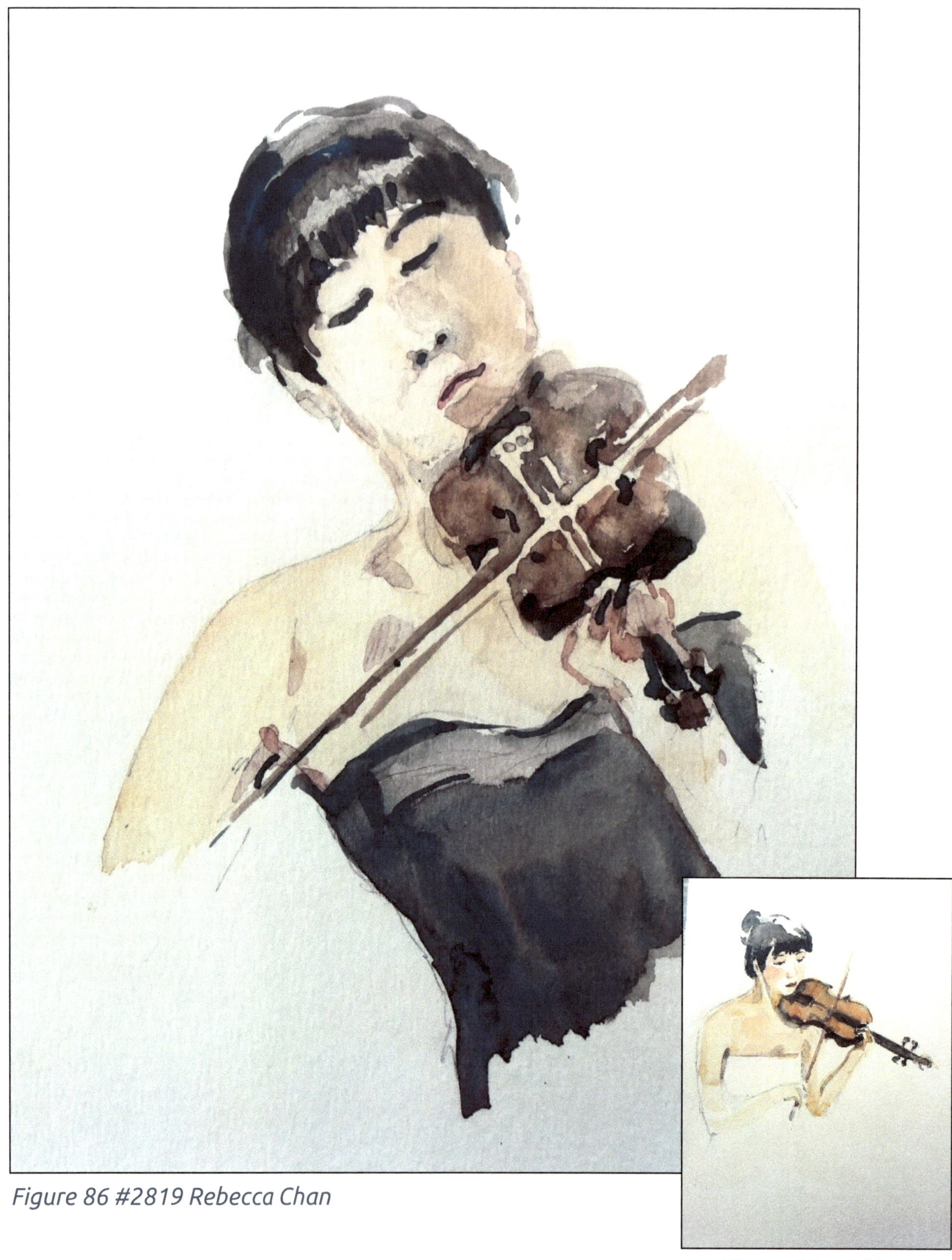

Figure 86 #2819 Rebecca Chan

Figure 85. #2907

Rebecca Chan

Rebecca Chan has medical as well as musical degrees and was a member of the Australian Chamber Orchestra from 2010 to 2015. She has since played as soloist with other leading Australian orchestras and is currently Assistant Leader with the Philharmonia Orchestra in London.

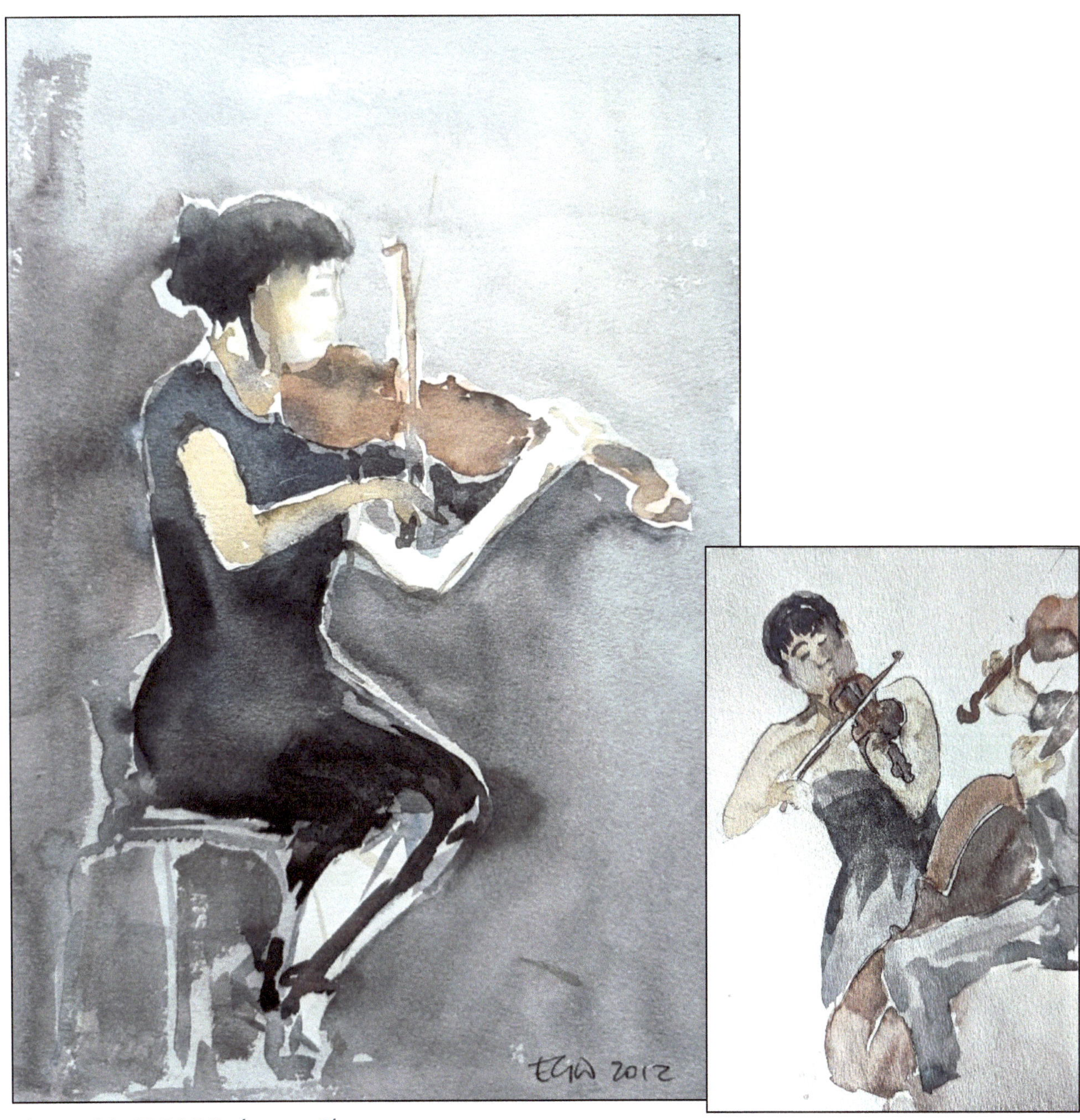

Figure 88 #2595 Rebecca Chan

Figure 87 #2820

Ilya Isakovich

This year (2024) Ilya Isakovich celebrated 20 years with the Australian Chamber Orchestra.

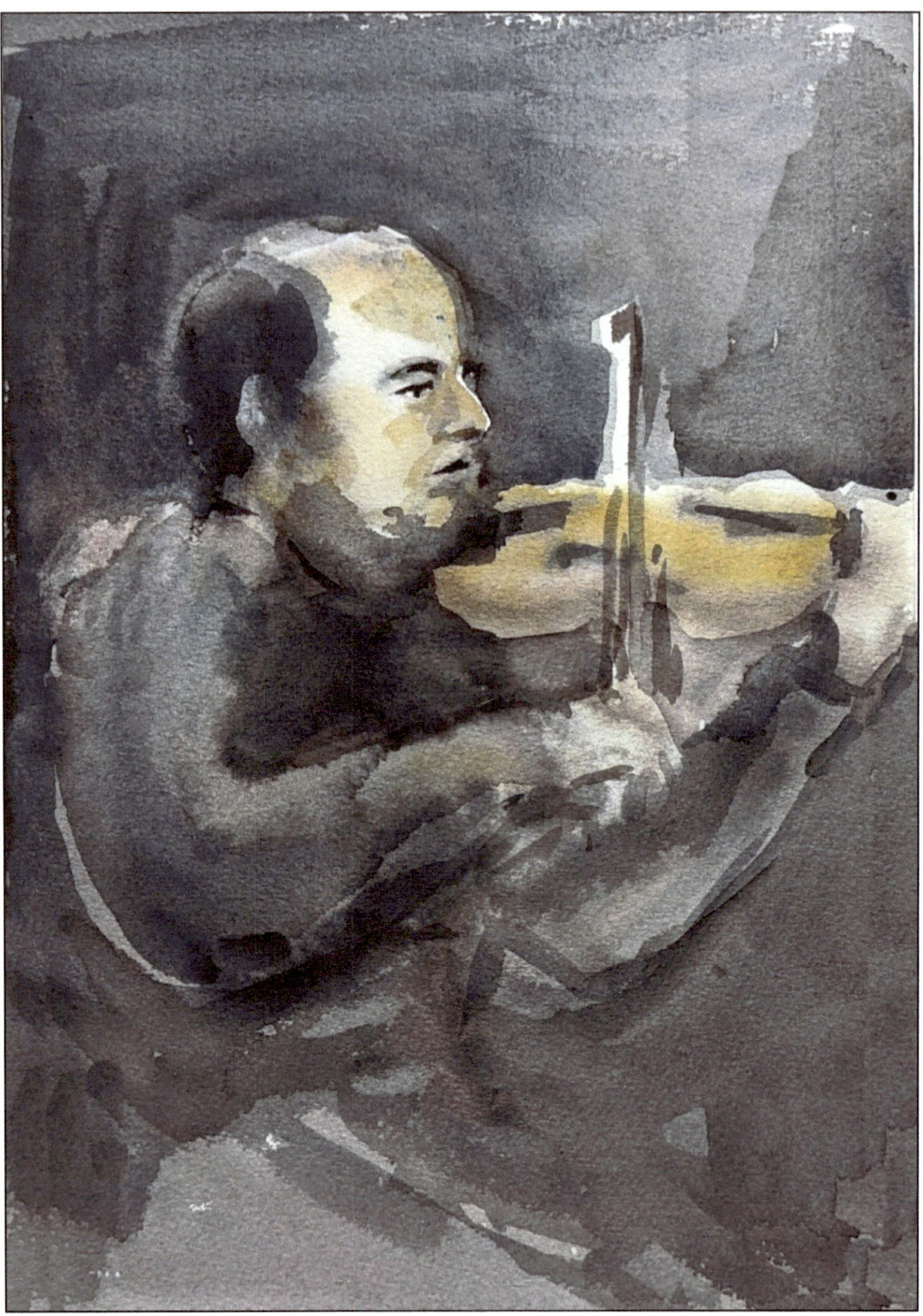

Figure 89. #2594 Ilya Isakovich, violin

Maya Savnik

Musicians playing with the Australian Chamber Orchestra come from all over the world. One of the more recent imports has been Maya Savnic from Slovenia. I first met Maya at the Maribor Music Festival while she was playing with the Slovenian Philharmonic Orchestra. I drew her in 2012 and 2014. She later joined the ACO and played with them until very recently, returning to Slovenia in 2024.

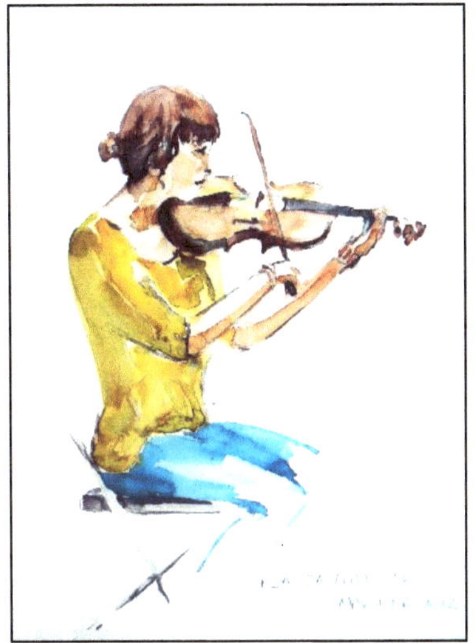

Figure 92. #2562 Maya, 2012

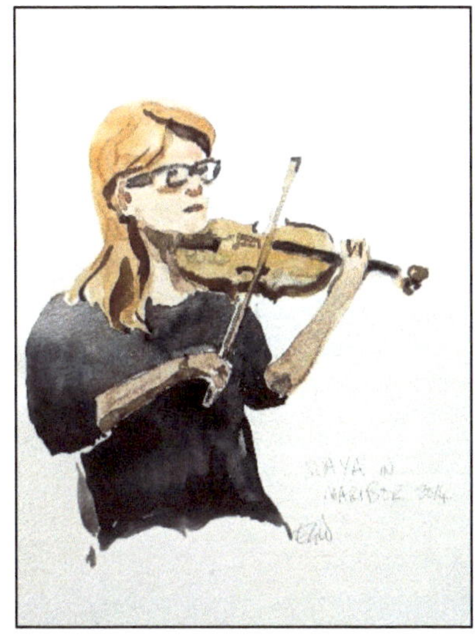

Figure 91 #2782 Maya, 2014

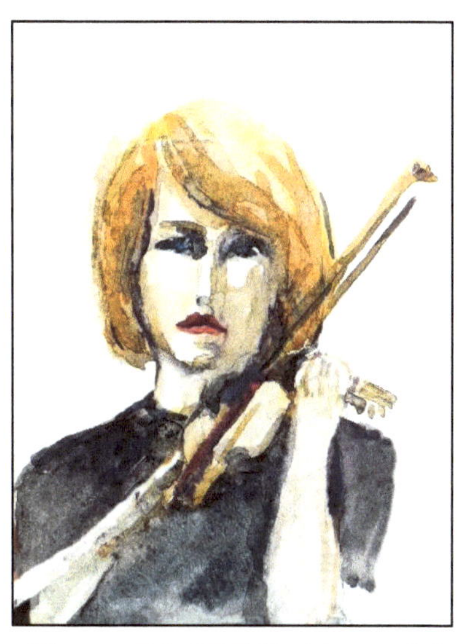

Figure 90 #3067 Maya, 2019

So far I have mainly painted musicians who are easily visible from the auditorium, but perhaps in future I will have the chance of painting those further back as well.

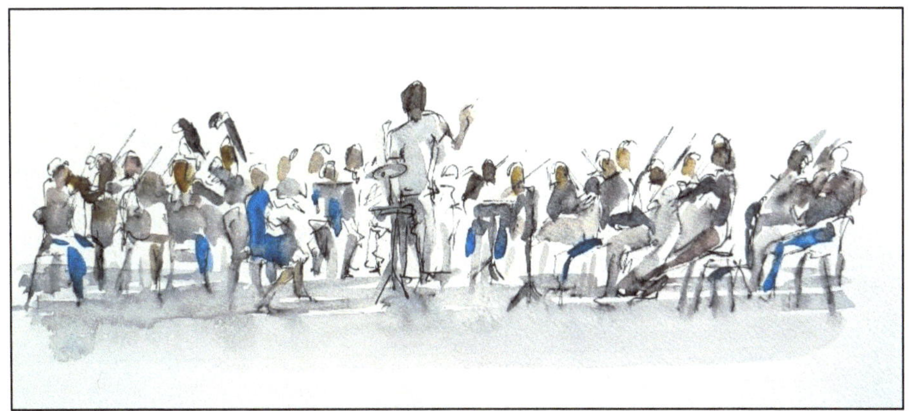

Figure 93. #2834 Richard Tognetti rehearsing with Orchestra.

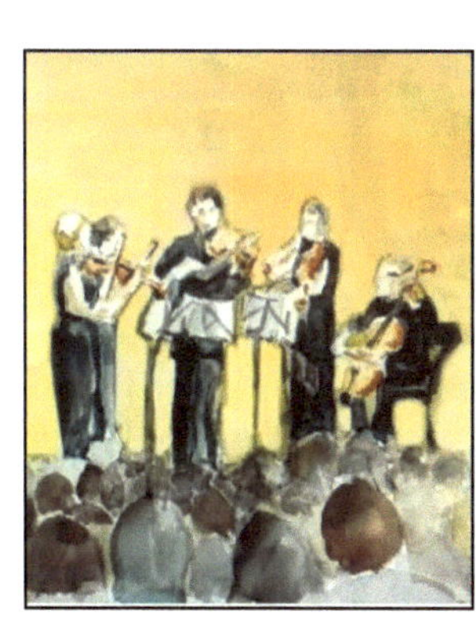

Figure 94. #2925 Aco members perform at the National Art School

Portrait of Satu Vänskä

In 2015 Satu Vänskä played a violin marathon in Maribor, the Sibelius Violin Concerto in D Minor, a work which has been called one of the most intense and difficult violin concertos ever written. Back home in Australia, after much thought I painted a contemplative portrait of Satu Vänskä for entry into the Archibald prize.

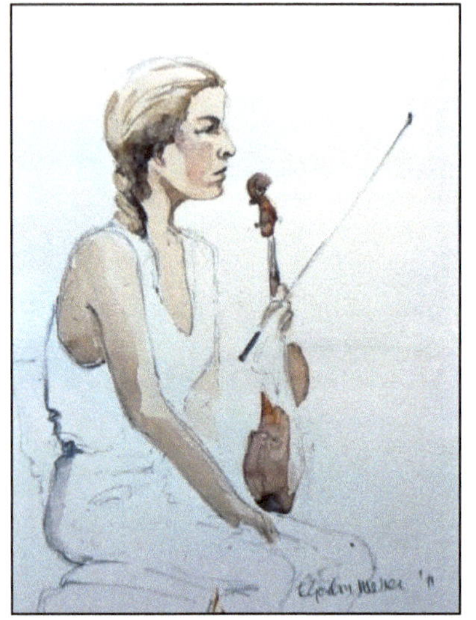

Figure 101. #2281 Satu

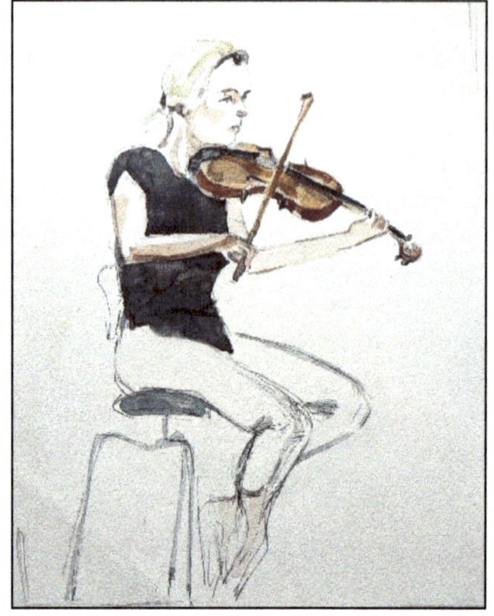

Figure 97 #2844

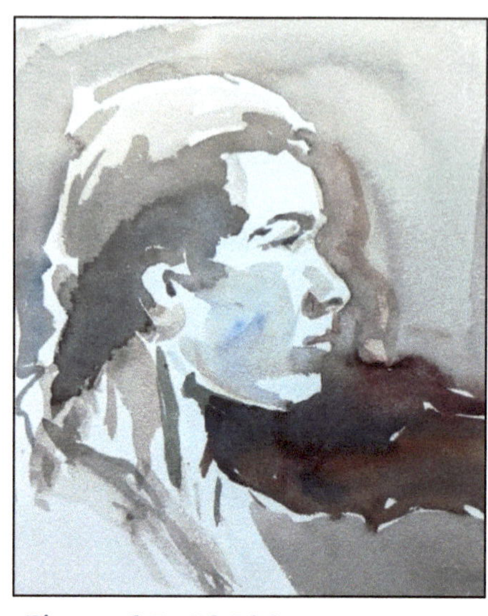

Figure 95. #2592

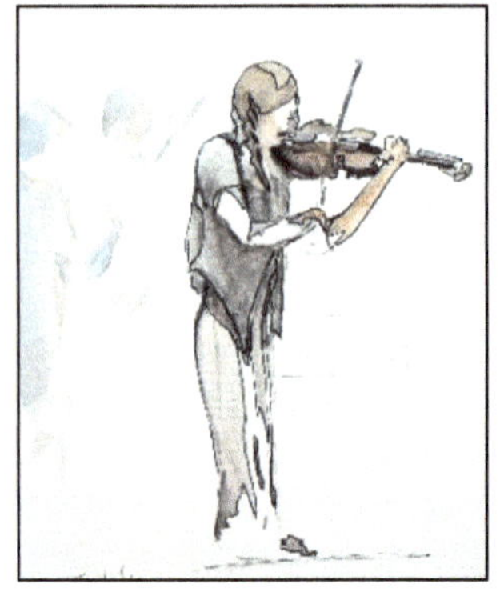

Figure 98. #2299

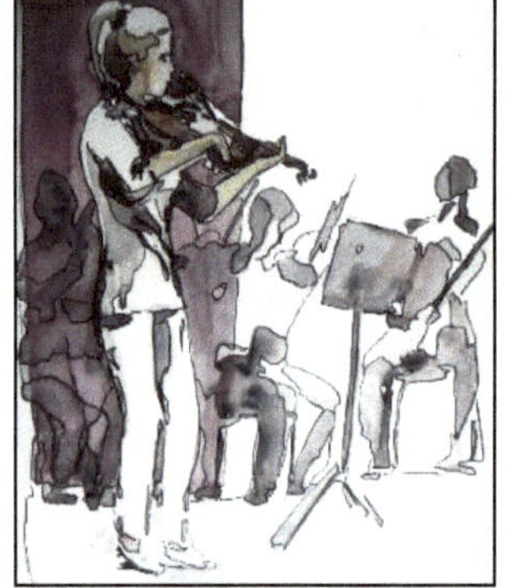

Figure 100. #2051

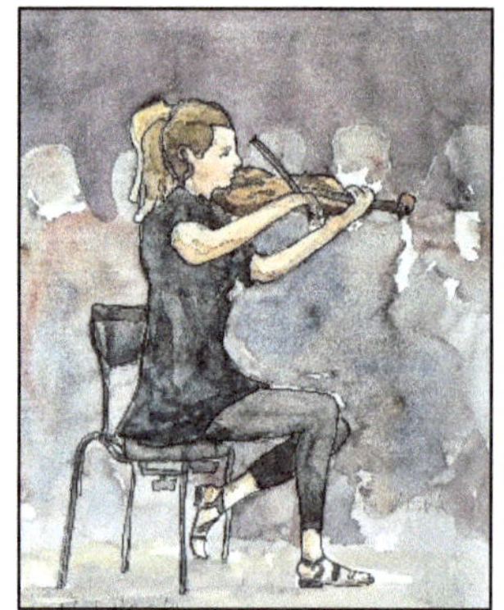

Figure 99. #2287

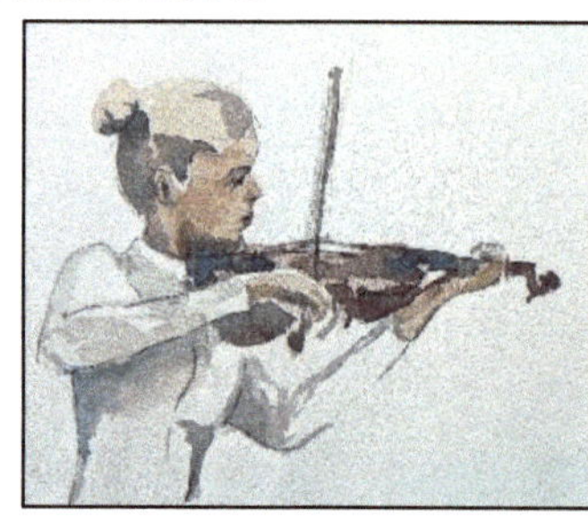

Figure 96. #2101

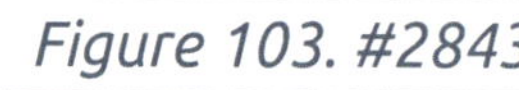

Figure 103. #2843

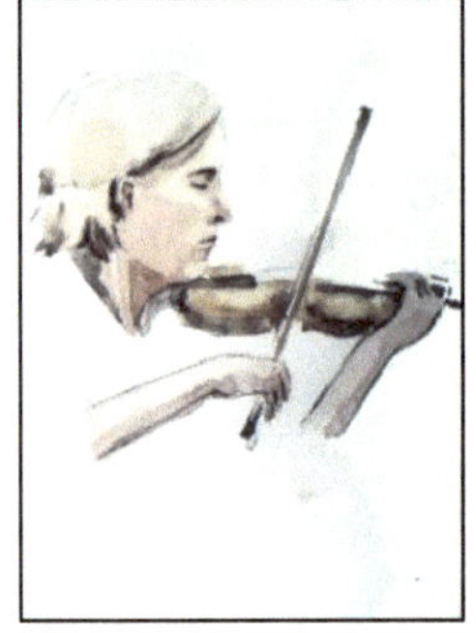

Figure 105 #1797

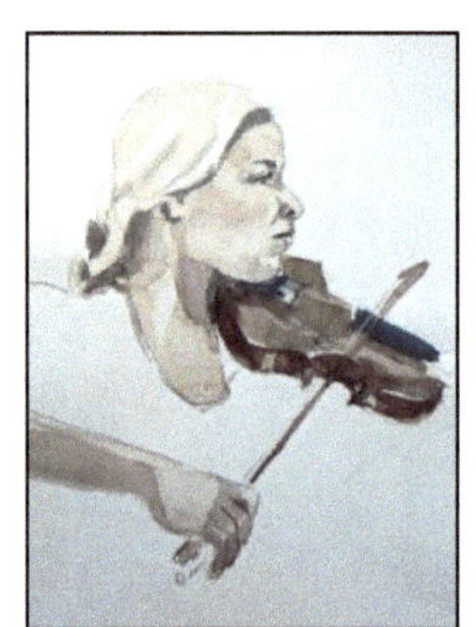

Figure 106. #2330

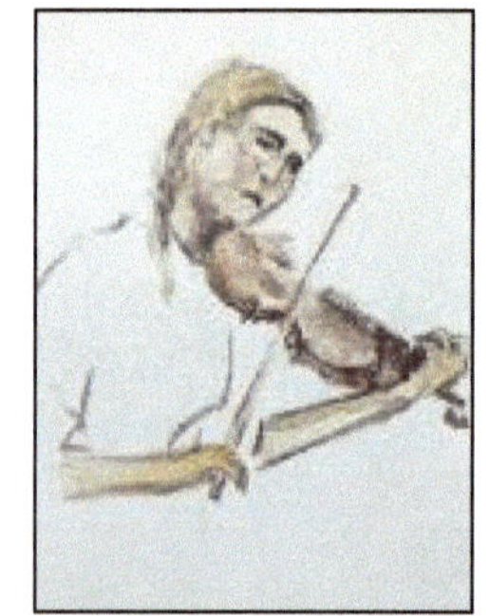

Figure 104. #2317

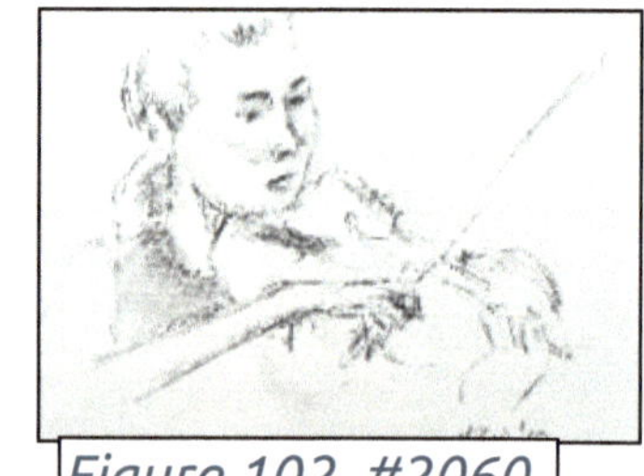

Figure 102. #2060

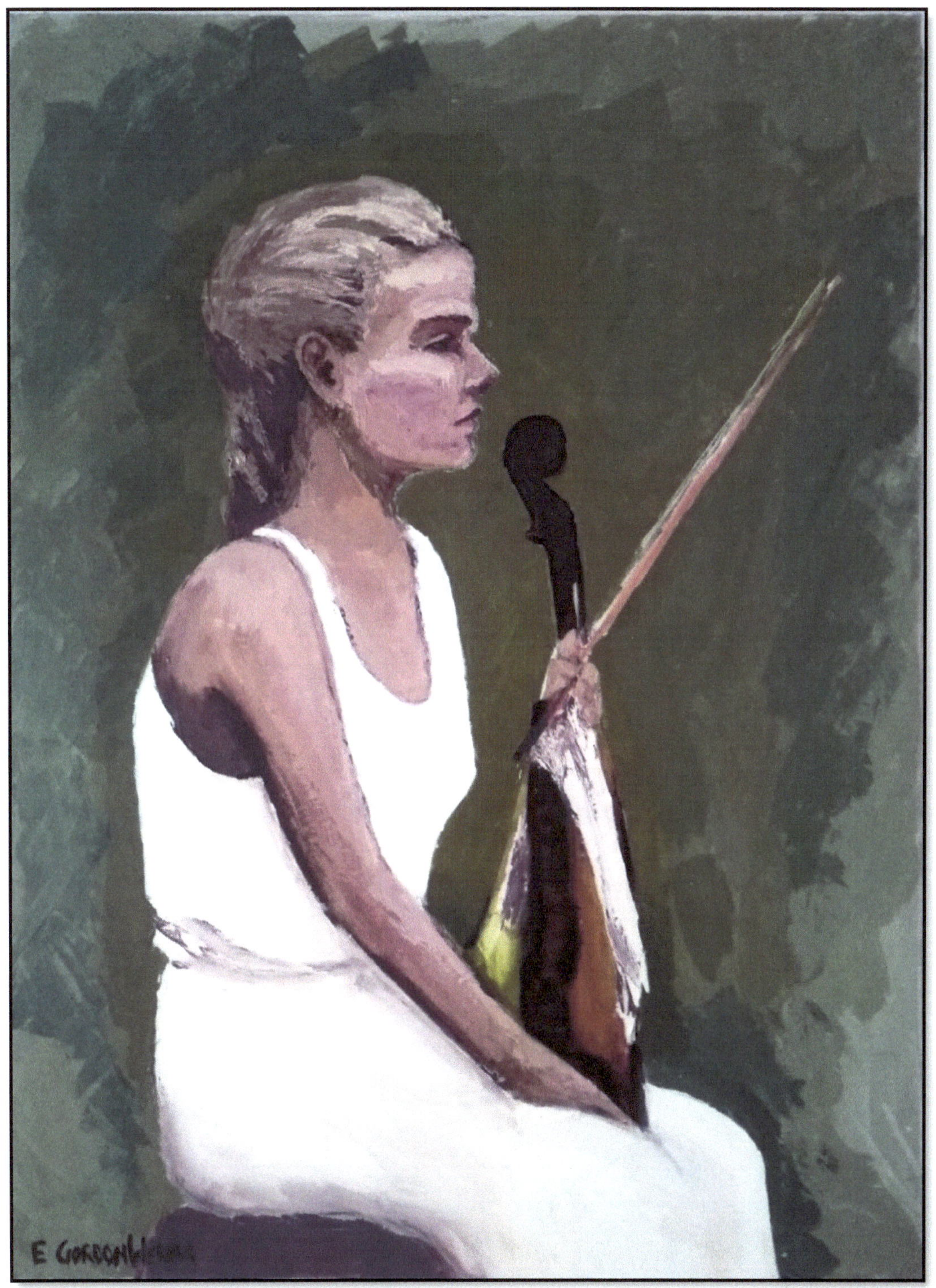

Figure 107. #2970 Satu Vänskä.2016. 102 x 76cm, acrylic/oil on canvas.

Musicians collaborating with the ACO

The Australian Chamber Orchestra works with many visiting musicians, poets, dancers and storytellers in their inovative performances. Some are from Australia, while others come on the long journey downunder just to play with them.

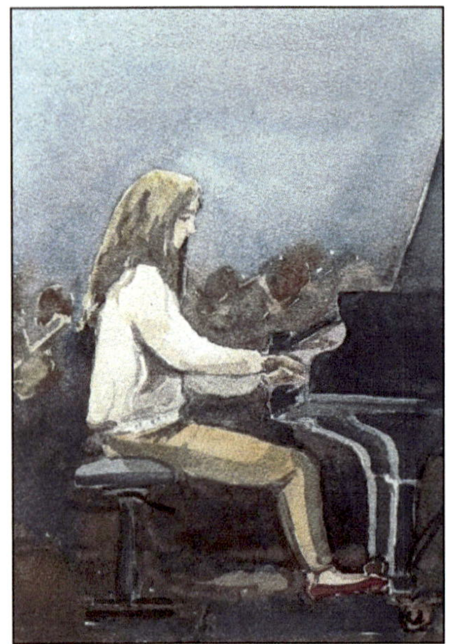

Figure 108. #2846 Polina Leschenko, piano

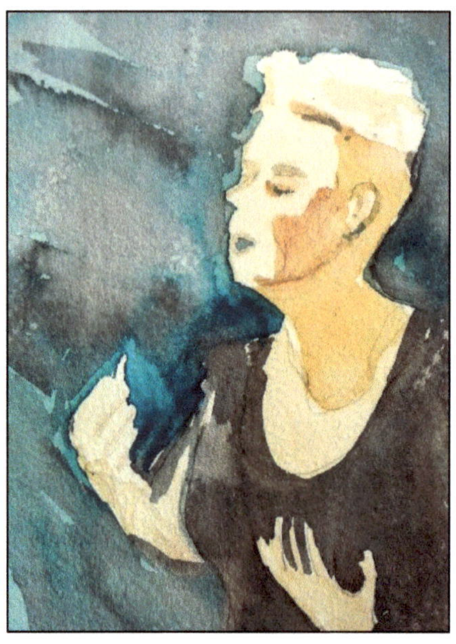

Figure 114. #2903 Katie Noonan

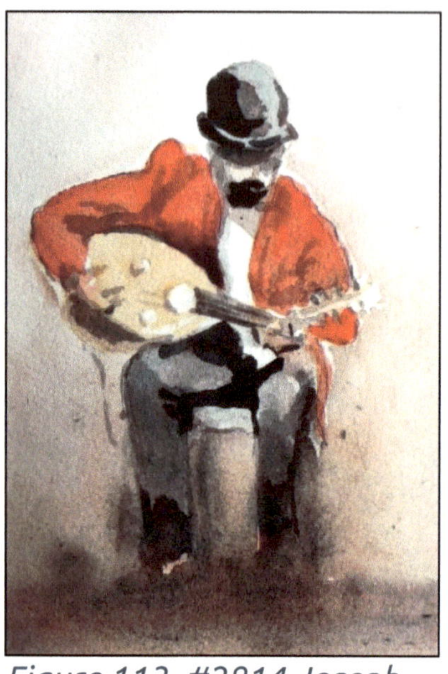

Figure 113. #2814 Joseph Tawadros, Oud.

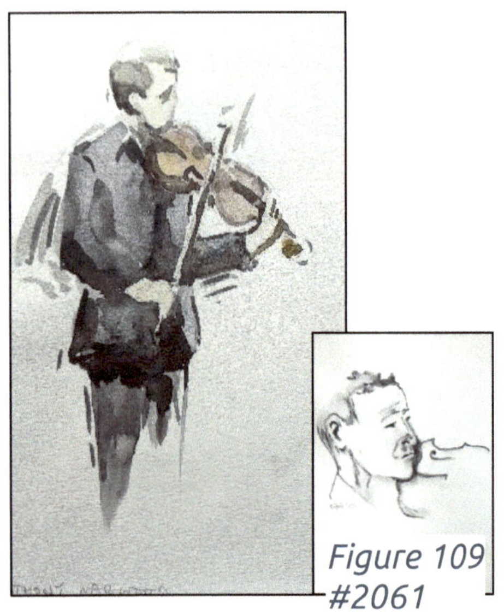

Figure 109 #2061

Figure 110. #2805. Anthony Marwood

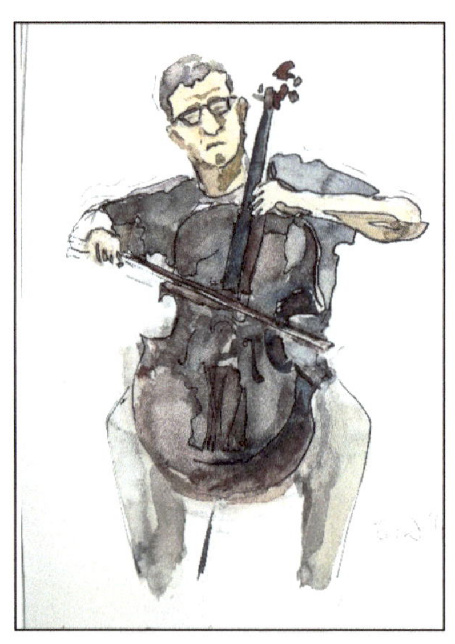

Figure 112 #2296 Giovanni Sollima

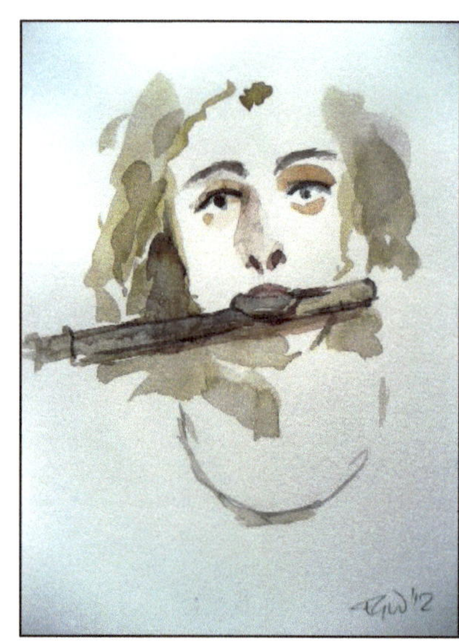

Figure 111 #2450 Jane Rutter

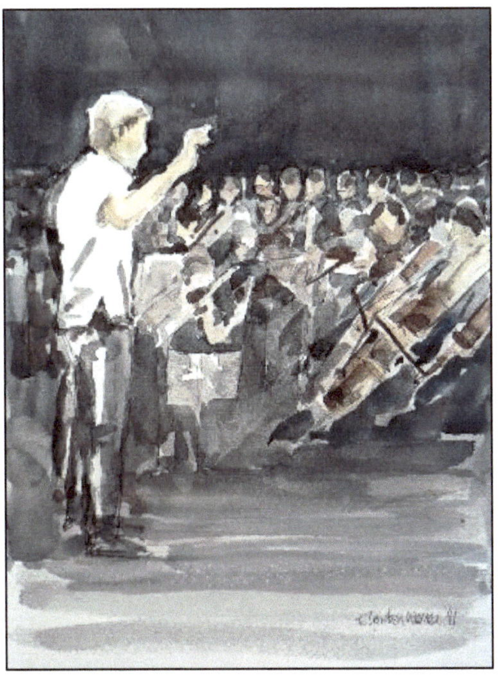

Figure 117. #2314

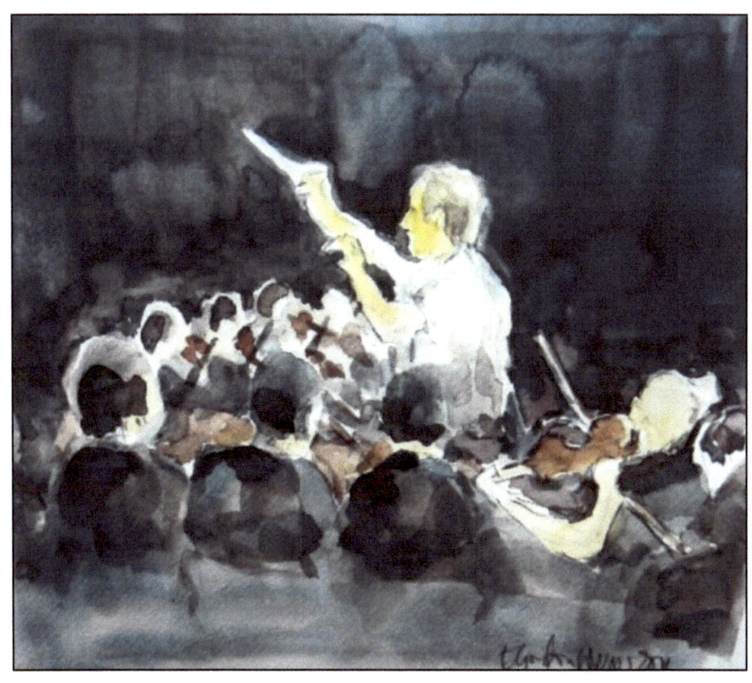

Figure 119. #2312 Richard Tognetti Conducting

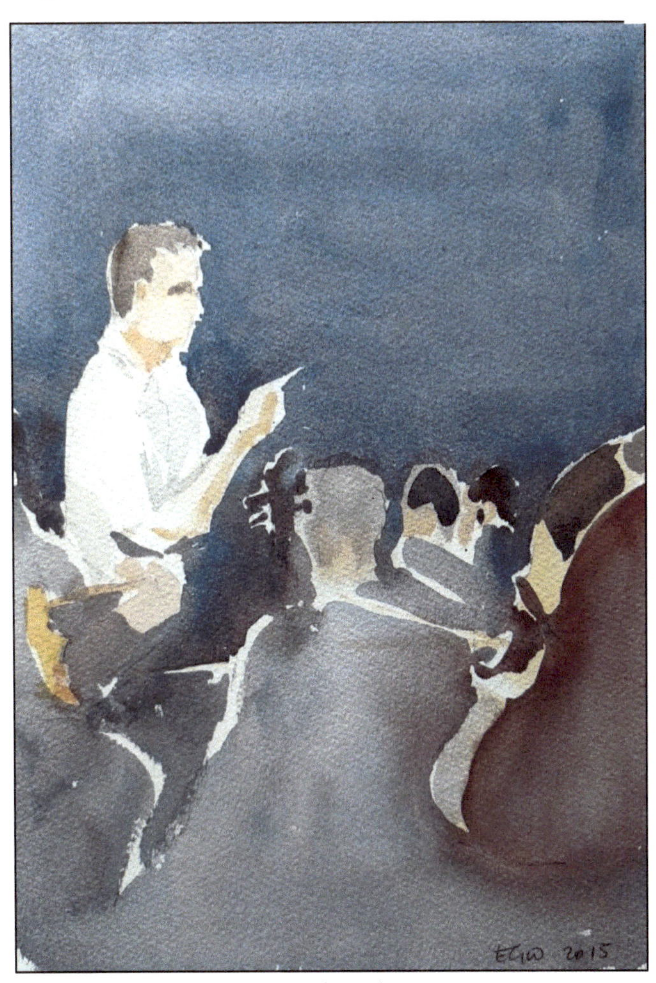

Figure 118. #2856 Richard Tognetti rehearsing with the orchestra.

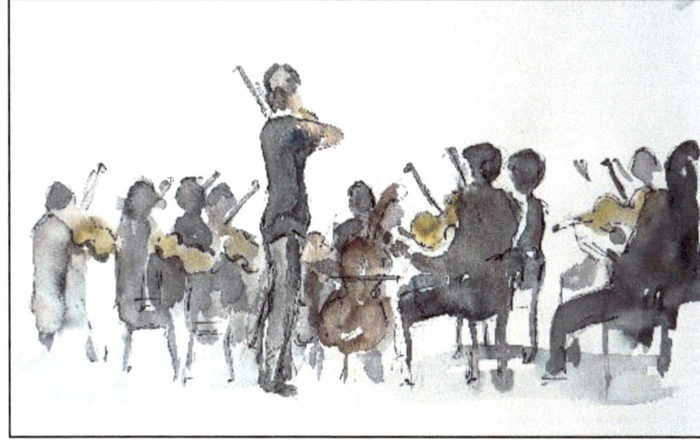

Figure 116. #2788

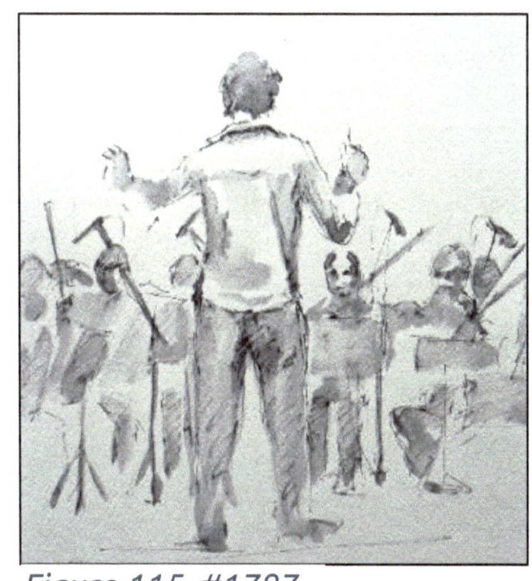

Figure 115. #1787

2020: A Sudden Change of Tempo

The world suddenly changed in 2020. We were in pandemic mode, Australia closed its borders, travelling was impossible, and we all wondered about our futures. My path to survival was to paint. I drew on all the sketches I had made of the ACO musicians and embarked on a series of abstract paintings. The ocean-green Sydney beaches edged themselves into these paintings. I spent eight years living in a beachside village in NSW and several of the Australian Chamber Orchestra are avid surfers, so perhaps it is not surprising.

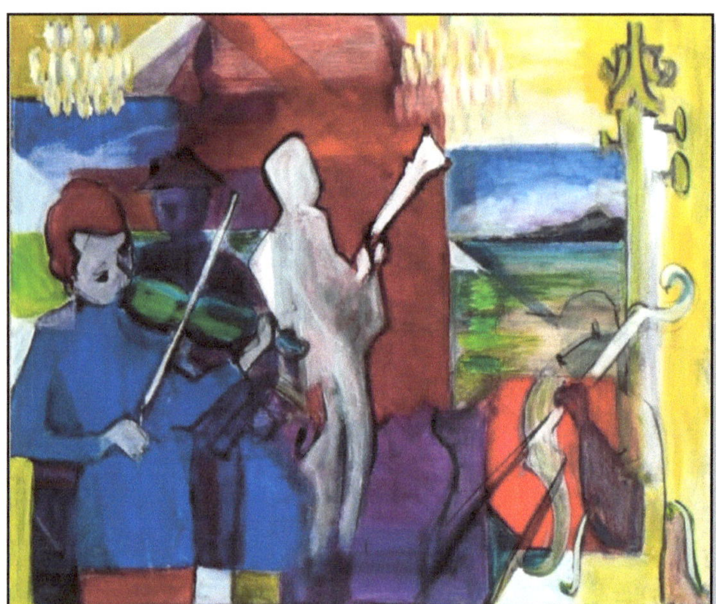

Musical Abstraction I

Chandeliers from Maribor, Sydney beaches and a guitarist drawn in a pub on the central coast made an appearance in *Musical Abstraction I*.

Figure 120 #3041 Musical Abstraction 1. 2020. 60 x 45.4 cm Acrylic on Canvas

Musical Abstraction II

The mirrored windows in Maribor's Kazina Hall feature in *Musical Abstraction II*.

Oh, and is that a penguin watching the musicians? Perhaps it is. I drew a lot of birds for a children's book in early 2020 and this one seems to have decided to explore elsewhere.

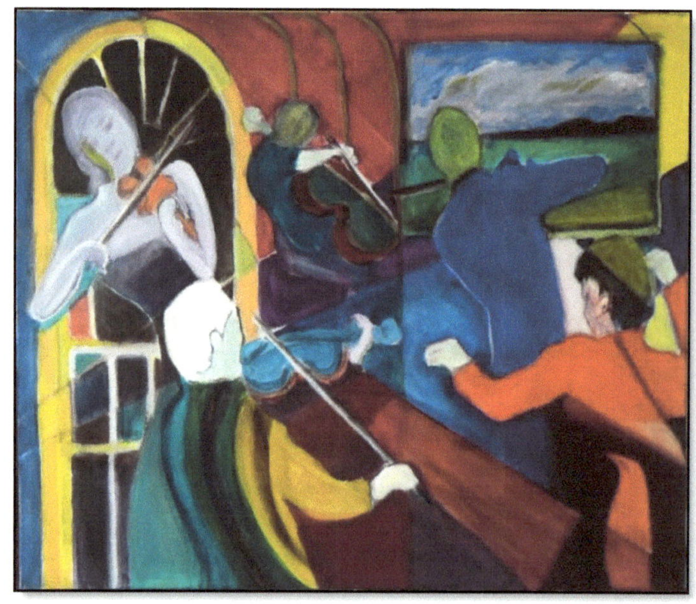

Figure 121 #3042 Musical Abstraction II. 2020. 60 x 50 cm Acrylic on Canvas

Musical Abstraction III

The sunbeams, remembered from a visit to London's St Paul's Cathedral where Yoko Ono had installed huge blond ropes high up on one of the side walls, stretching them diagonally down to the opposite side where they were secured by rocks. When you entered the cathedral you thought you saw sunbeams streaming through a window. Then you realised there were no windows there.

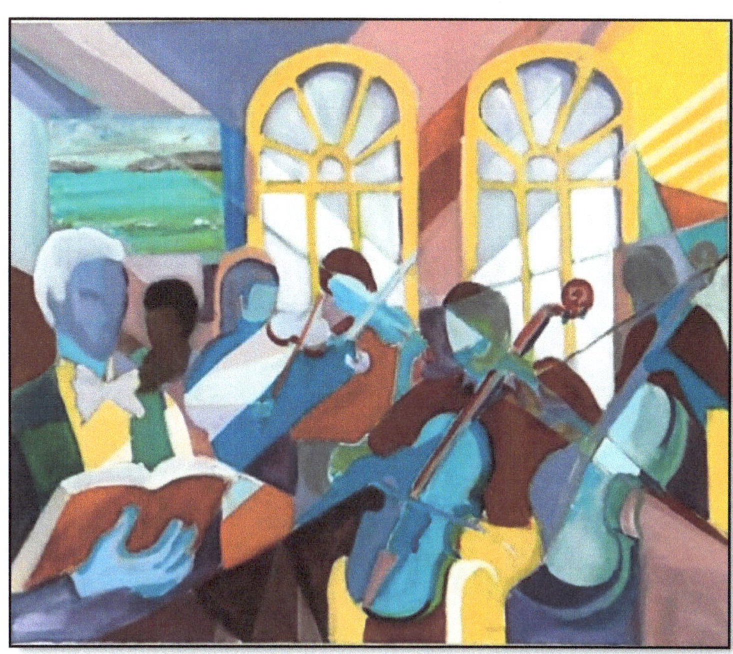

Figure 122 #3043 Musical Abstraction III 2020. 60 x 50 cm Acrylic on Canvas

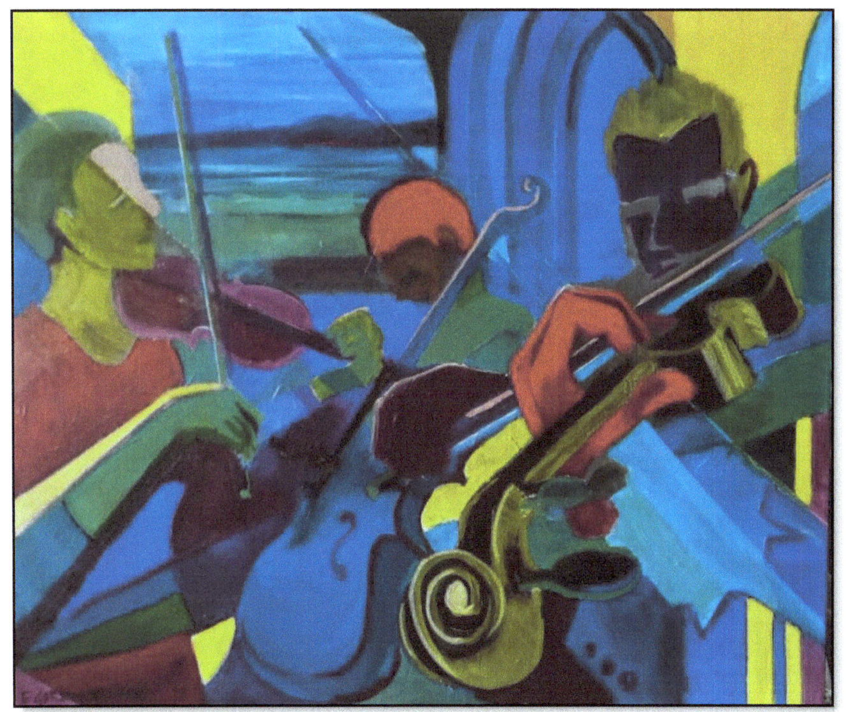

Figure 123. #3044 Musical Abstraction IV. 2020. 60 x 50 cm Acrylic on Canvas

Musical Abstraction IV

The Maribor Cathedral, streaming light, the players playing.

I didn't plan the paintings in this set of abstractions, somehow they just painted themselves. I would start off with a blotch of colour on a canvas and see where it led me. As the series expanded, each painting got more abstract.

Musical Abstraction IV

The sunshine enters *Musical Abstraction V* and almost takes it over. The sunbeams enter from two directions, though a Maribor inspired mirrored window and from high up on the wall where the Choir of London sing their song. A violin dreams of the beach.

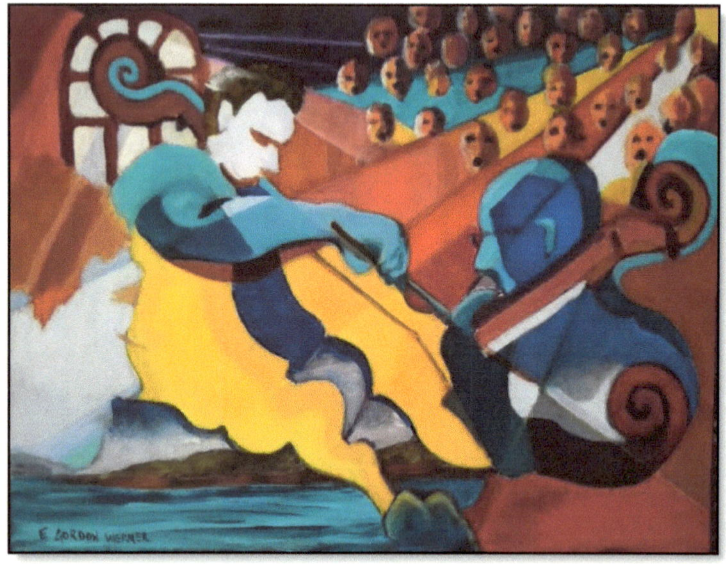

Figure 125 #3045 Musical Abstraction V. 2020. 60 x 45.5 cm Acrylic on Canvas

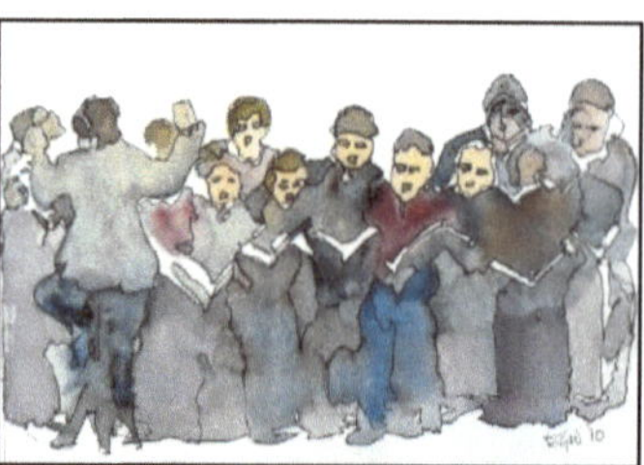

Figure 124 #2105 Richard Tognetti and the Choir of London in Maribor

The 1743 Guarneri del Gesù violin played by Richard Tognetti was the inspiration behind *Striped Violin* while *The Blond Girl Plays Violin* came as if from a dream.

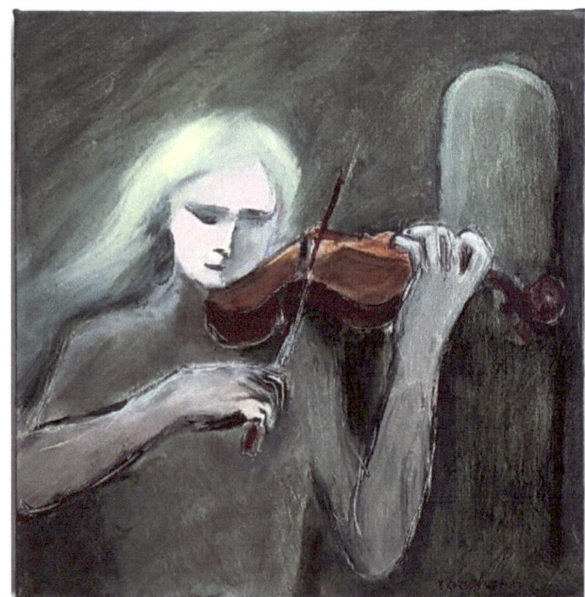

Figure 127 #3116 Blond Girl plays Violin 2023 51x51 cm Acrylic on Canvas

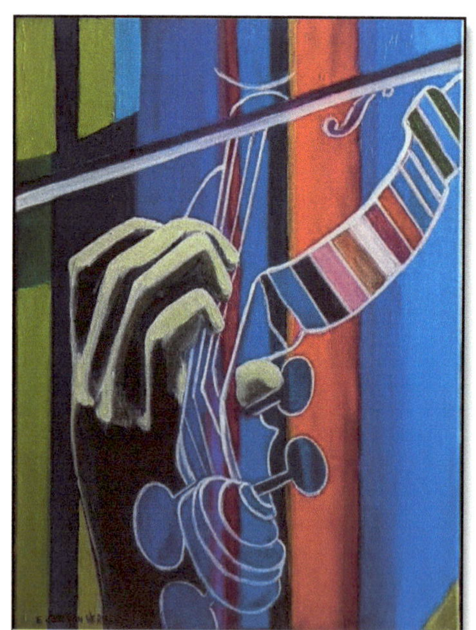

Figure 126. #3112. Striped Violin. 2023 46x60.5cm Acrylic on Canvas

2022 and the ACO stream videos

A new year dawned, and The Australian Chamber Orchestra were producing 'home casts', videos made during the lockdowns and put online to keep their audiences entertained (and, I assume, to keep themselves sane.) My paintbrush started producing less abstract ACO-centred images. They were colour compositions. I made sketches and plans for these works, but they always changed as I painted. The one constant was the orchestra. They appeared on every canvas.

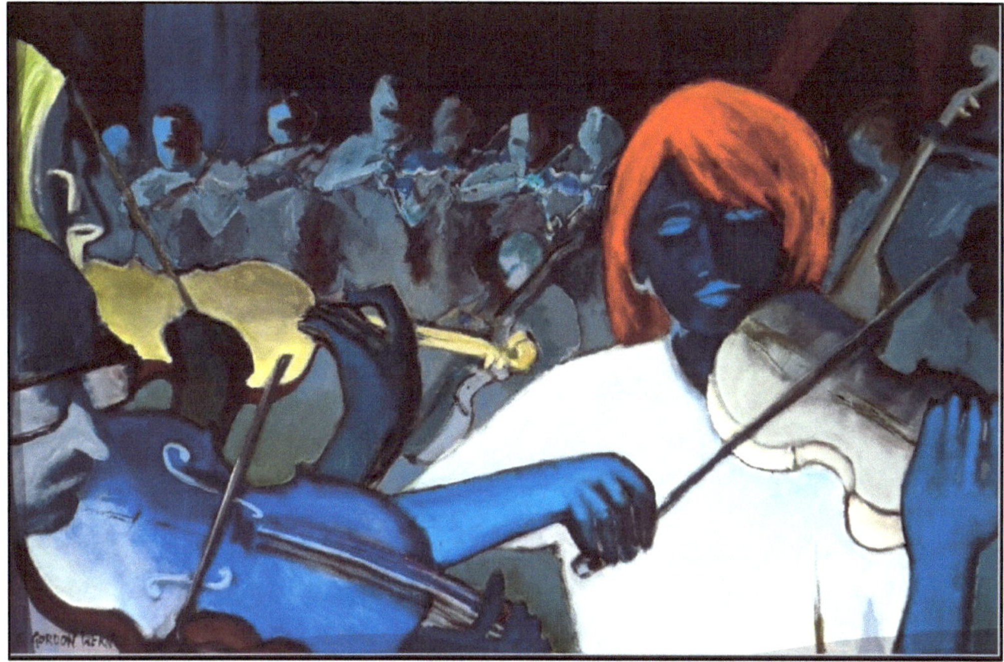

Figure 128. #3070 Red haired violinist. 2021. 90x60 cm. Acrylic on Canvas.

ACO After Dark

The multi-talented Australian Chamber Orchestra play not only in concert halls and at festivals; they play in nightclubs as well, in a series called ACO After Dark.

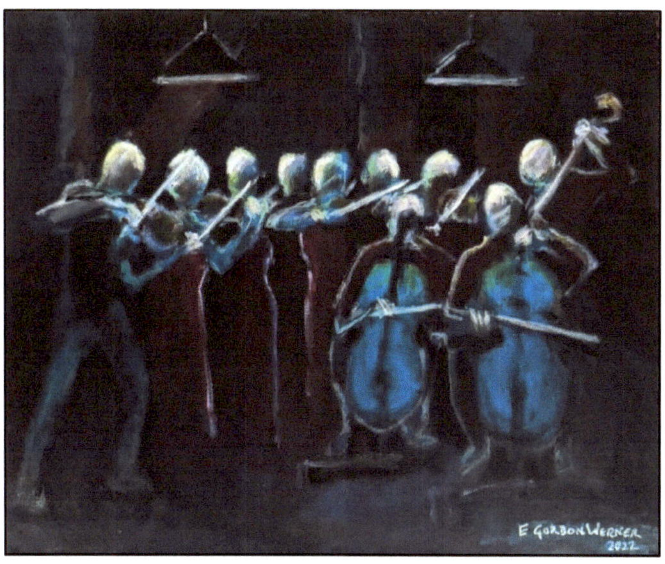

Figure 129 #3072 ACO After Dark. 2021. 40x50cm. Acrylic on Canvas.

Painting a Viola Player in Wood

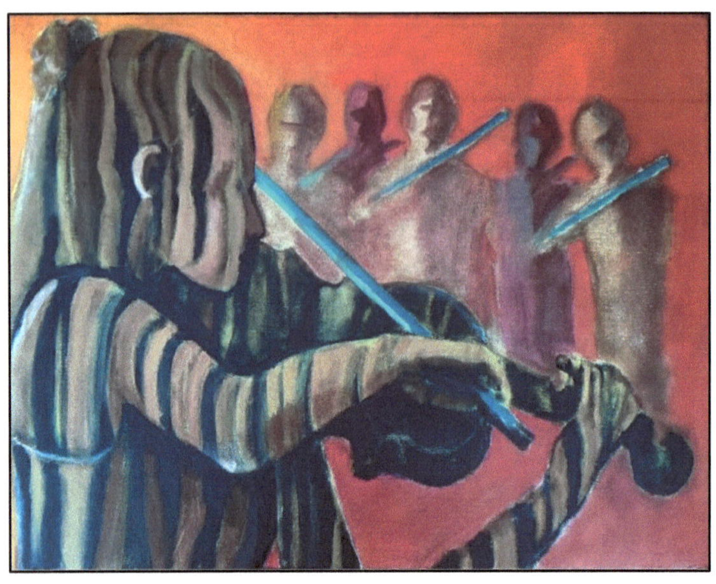

Figure 130 #3074. Wooden viola player. 2021. 45x60cm. Acrylic on Canvas.

Many years ago I aquired a wooden figurine of a woman meditating, or perhaps it is the Buddah meditating. It is from Bali, carved out of hardwood by very clever hands and it is one of my favourite objects. It has moved with me on my many moves over the years. This wooden statue transformed itself into a viola player in *Wooden Viola Player*. This painting took time and I dispaired of it working, nearly painting over the whole thing several times. But suddenly there she was, the viola player, solo, with her colleagues joining in from behind her.

Trio: Bass, viola, Violin

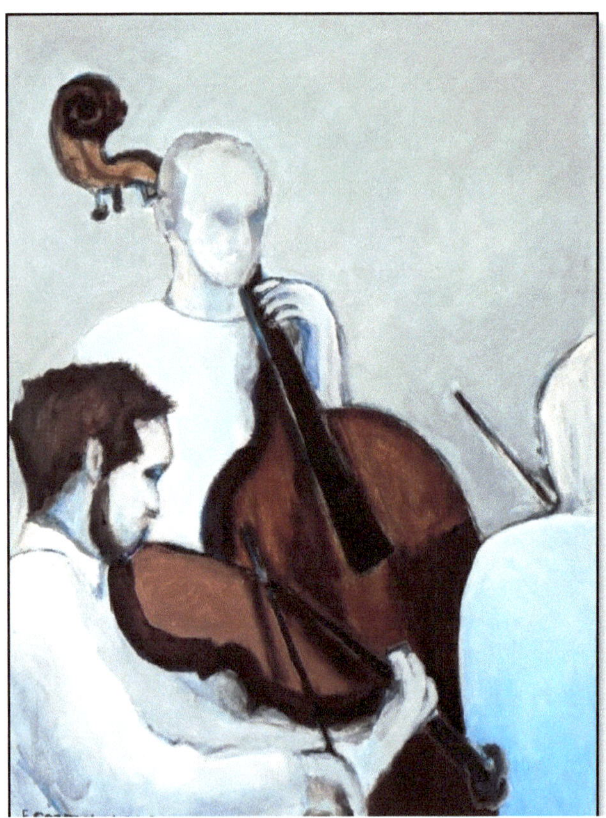

Figure 132 #3076. Bass, viola, violin. 2022. 45x60cm. Acrylic on Canvas.

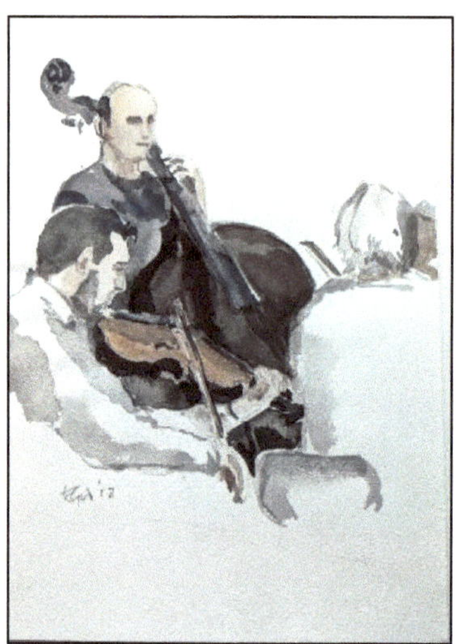

Figure 131 #2573. Christopher Moore, Maxime Bibeau, Helene Rathbone

Players on Yellow

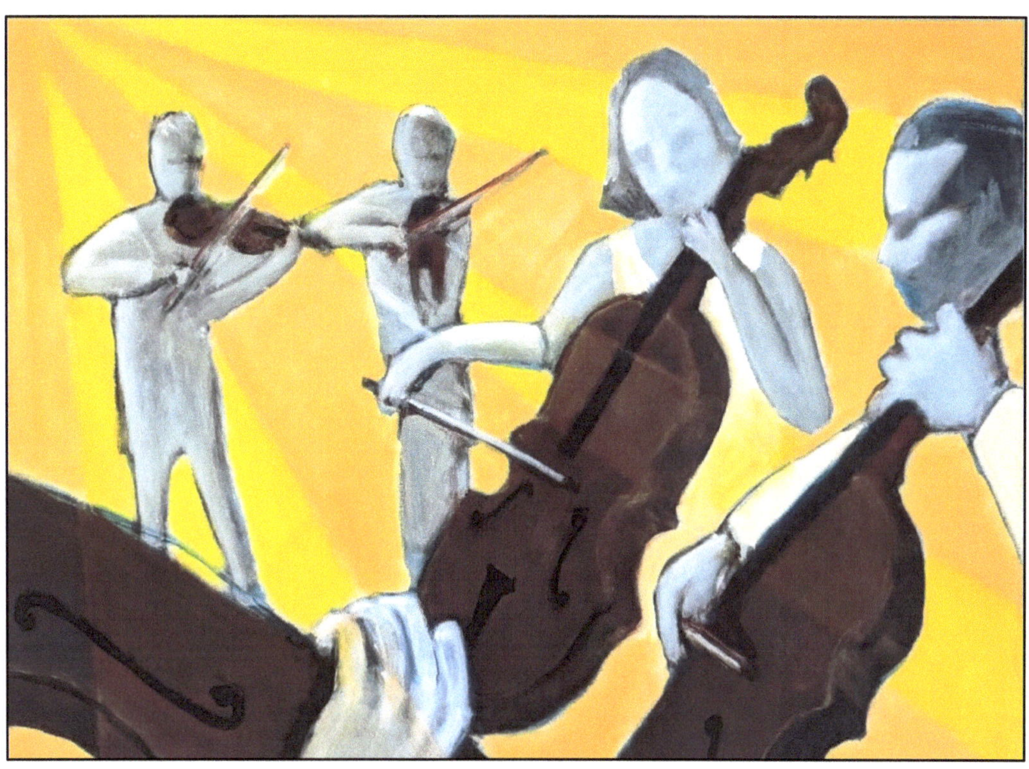

Figure 133. #3077 Players on Yellow. 2022 45x60cm Acrylic on Canvas.

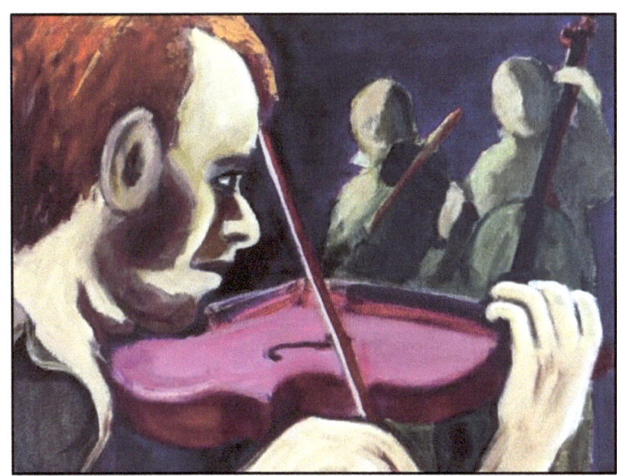

Figure 134. #3081 Pink Violin 2. 2022 30x40cm Acrylic on Canvas

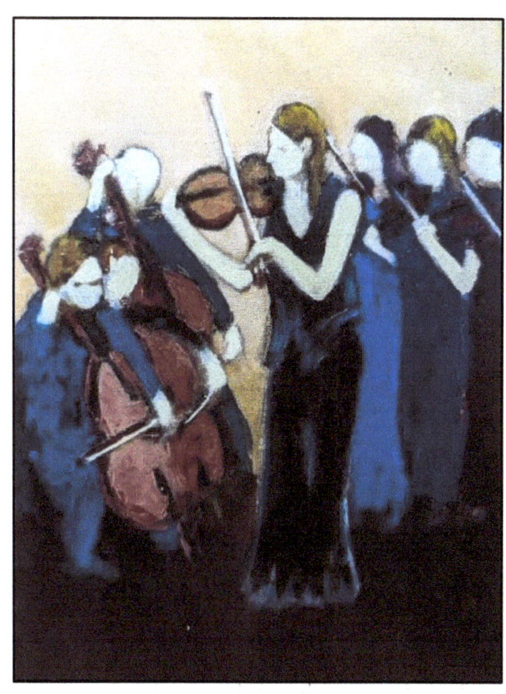

Figure 135. Soloist 2022. 30x40cm Acrylic on Canvas.

Conductor and Orchestra

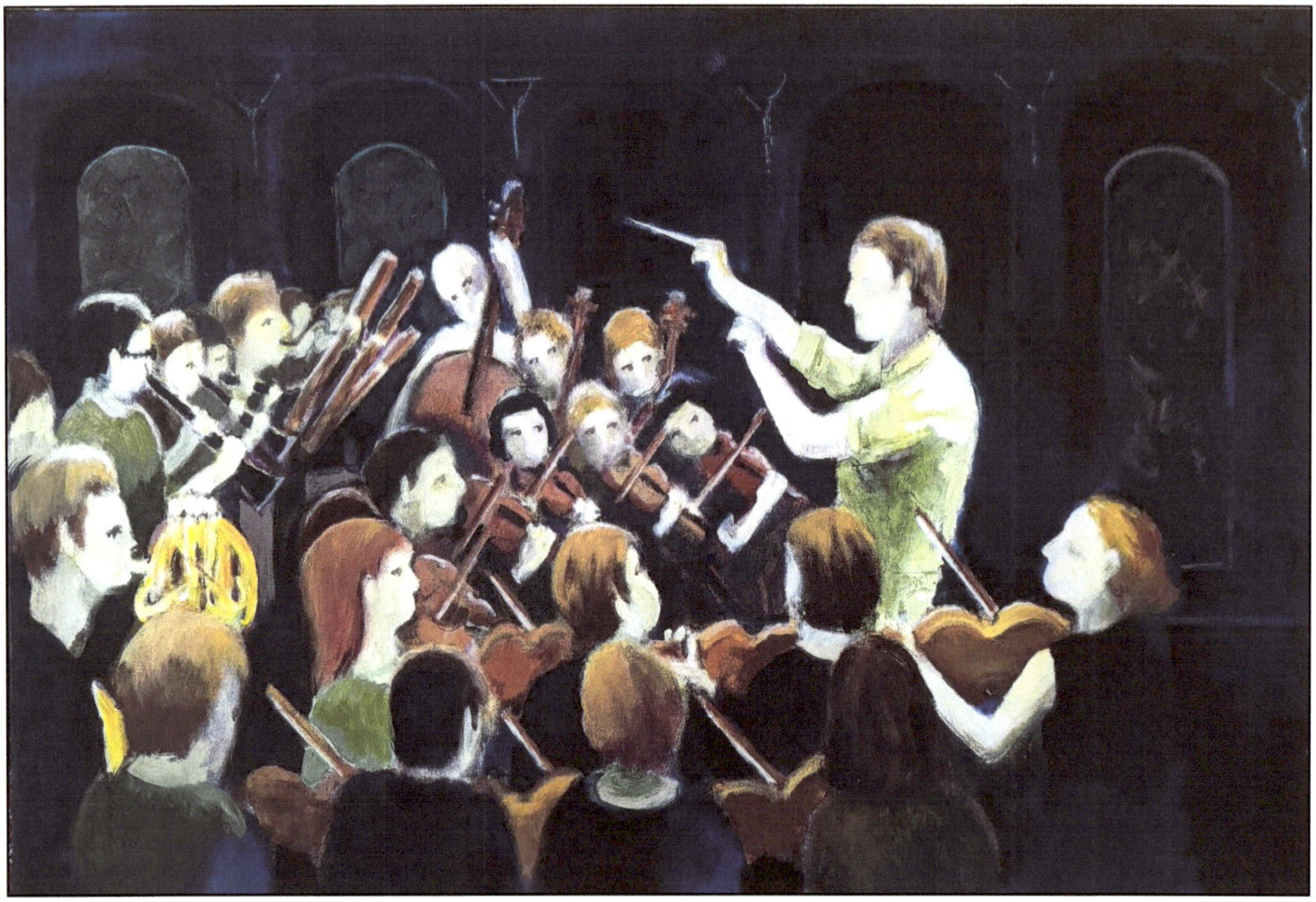

Figure 136. #3079 Conductor with Orchestra. 2022. 50x75cm Acrylic on Canvas

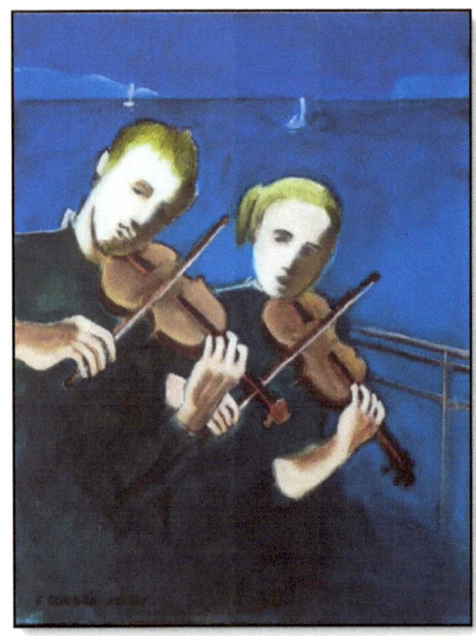

Figure 138. #3078 Players on the Manly Ferry

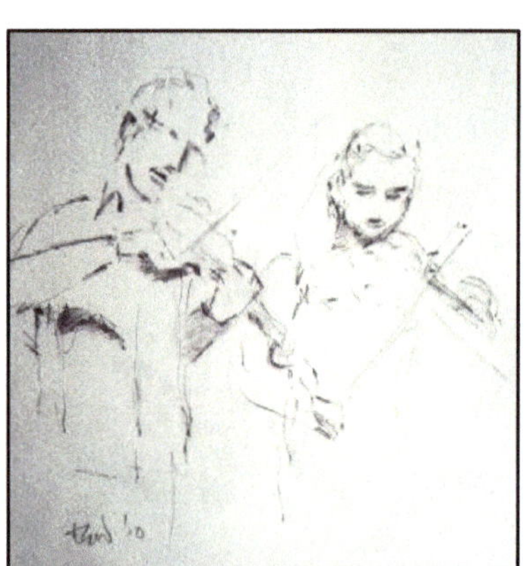

Figure 137. #2092 Richard and Satu in 2010 (my favourite sketch)

Blue Cellist

Musicians practise so much before audiences hear a note, first by themselves and then with the group. This focus is a special talent.

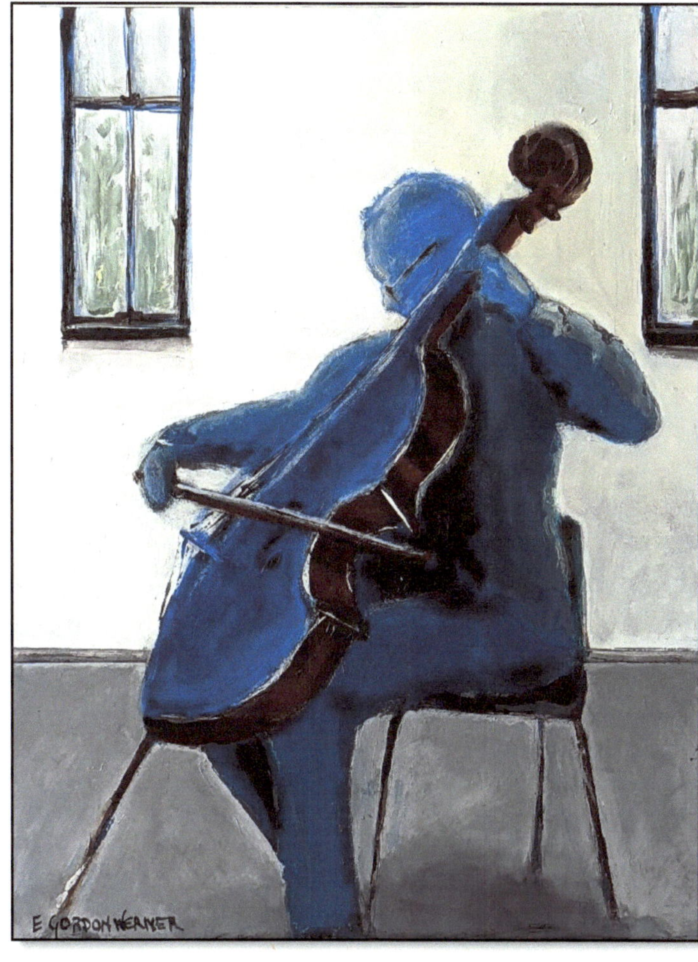

Figure 139 #3111 Blue Cellist: Timo-Veikko Valve. 2023. 45x60cm. Acrylic on Wood.

Violinist with Chagall

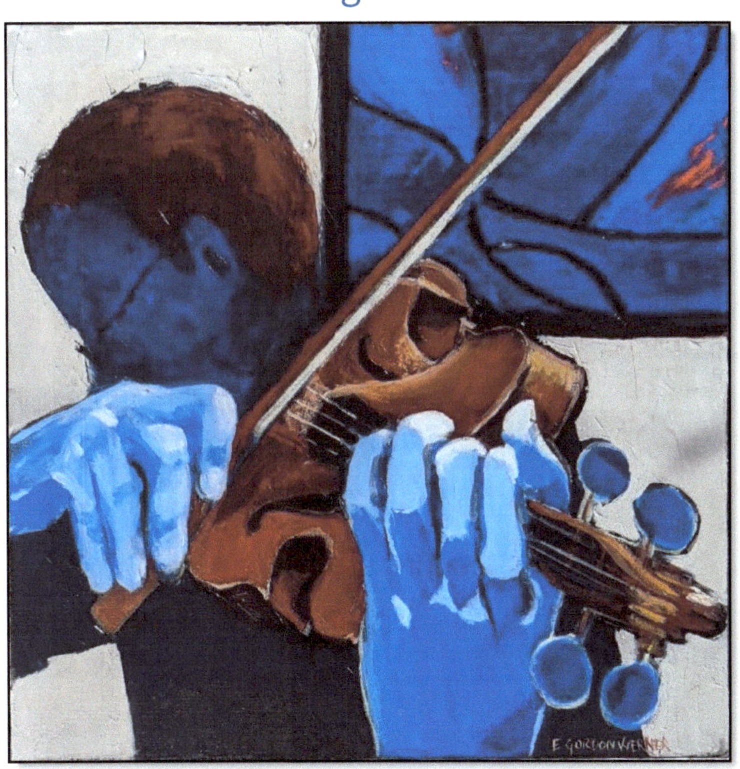

Once you see Chagall blue glass windows like those in St Stephen's Church in Mainz, you never forget them. Another memorable set of blue windows are the Prisoners of Conscience windows in Salisbury Cathedral. Memories of both are in *Violinist with Chagall window.*

Figure 140. #3114 Violinist with Chagall window. 2023 51x51cm Acrylic on Canvas

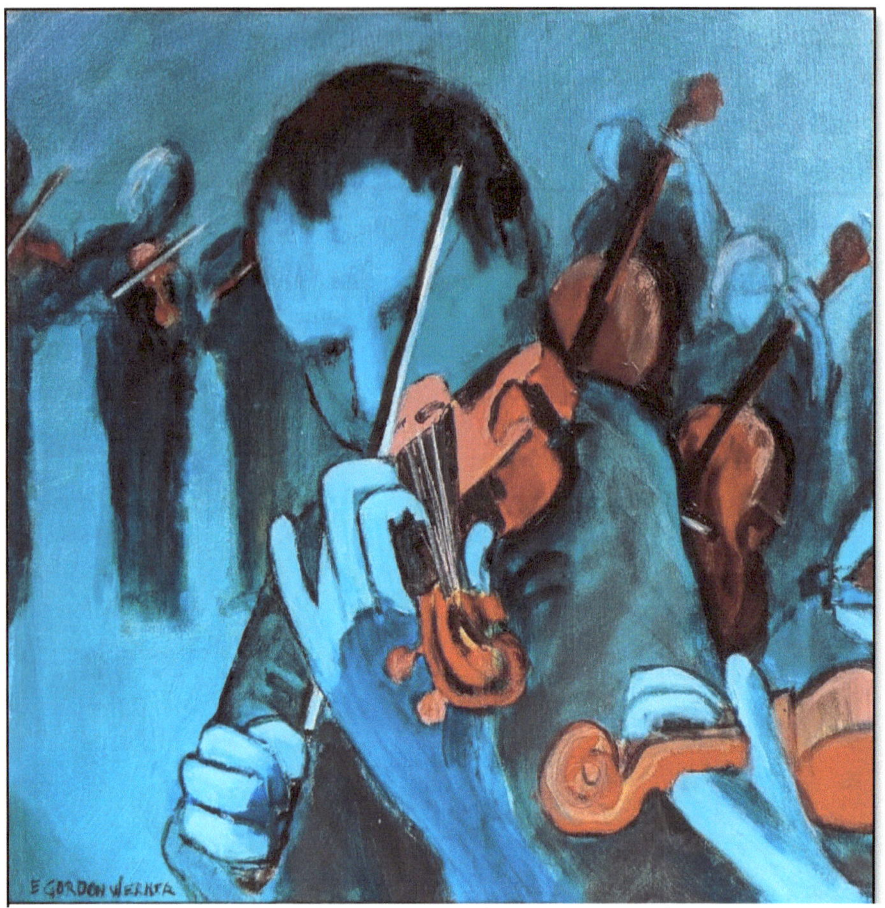

Figure 141. #3115 Violinist in Southern Ocean Blue 51x51cm Acrylic on Canvas

Southern Ocean Blue

The colour Southern Ocean Blue is very relevant for Australia where the seas are this colour throughout the year.

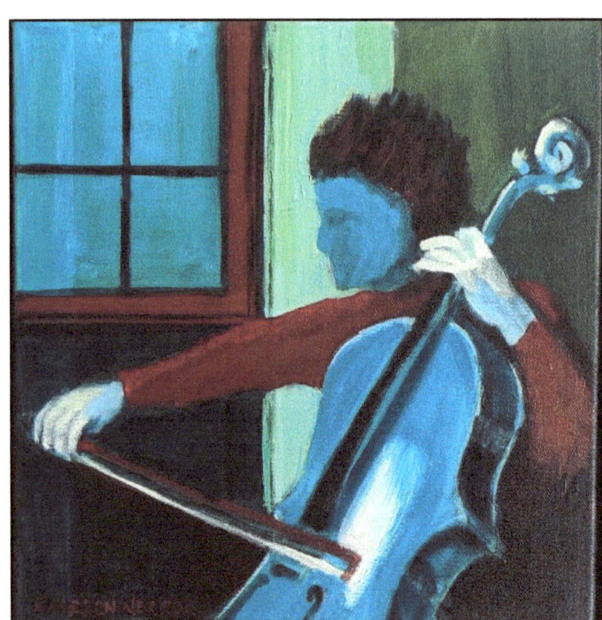

Figure 142. #3121 Violinist and window. 30x30cm Acrylic on Canvas

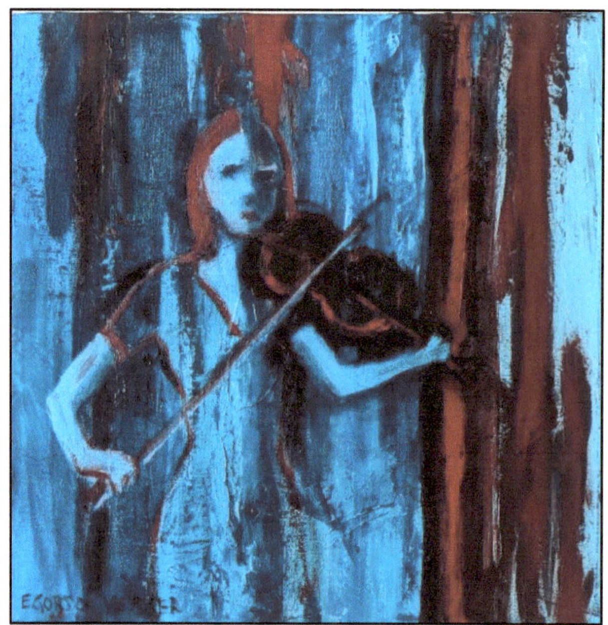

Figure 143. #3120 Violinist in Ocean Blue and Red 2023 30x30cm Acrylic on Canvas

Players in Rising Waters

As an artist who is also an environmental scientist, the change in climate we are witnessing is not unexpected. However, it is not easy to watch the distress of climate scientists as disinformation muddies the waters and confuses the public.

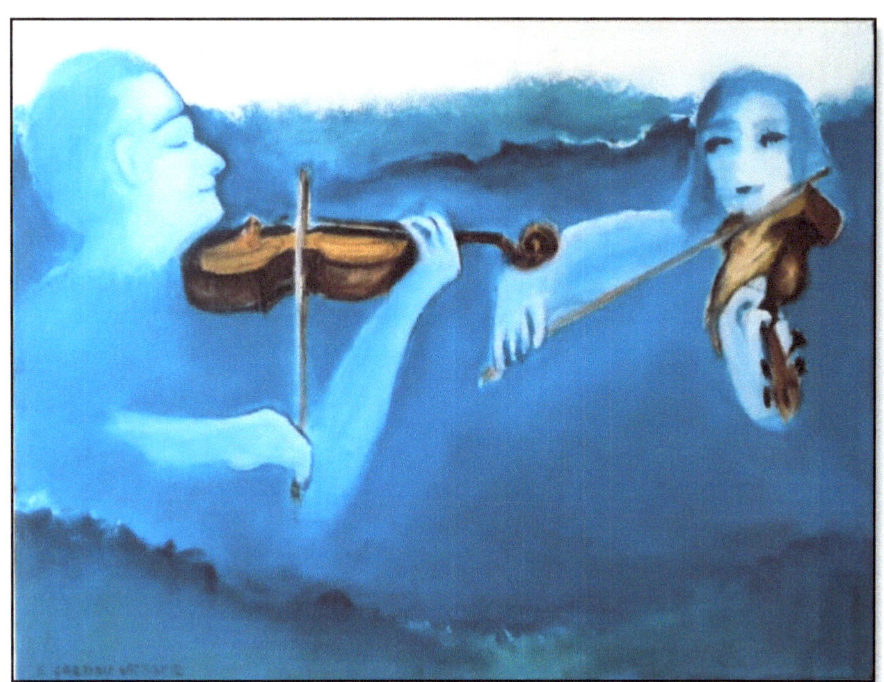

Figure 145. #3118 Players in rising waters I. 2023 46x60.5 cm. Acrylic on Canvas

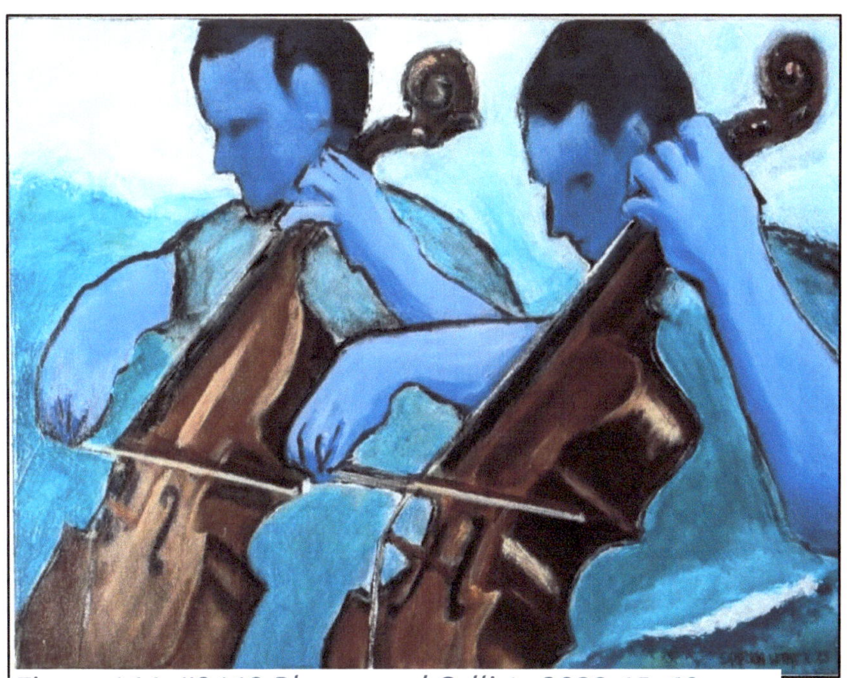

Figure 144. #3113 Blue armed Cellists 2023 45x60cm Acrylic on Canvas

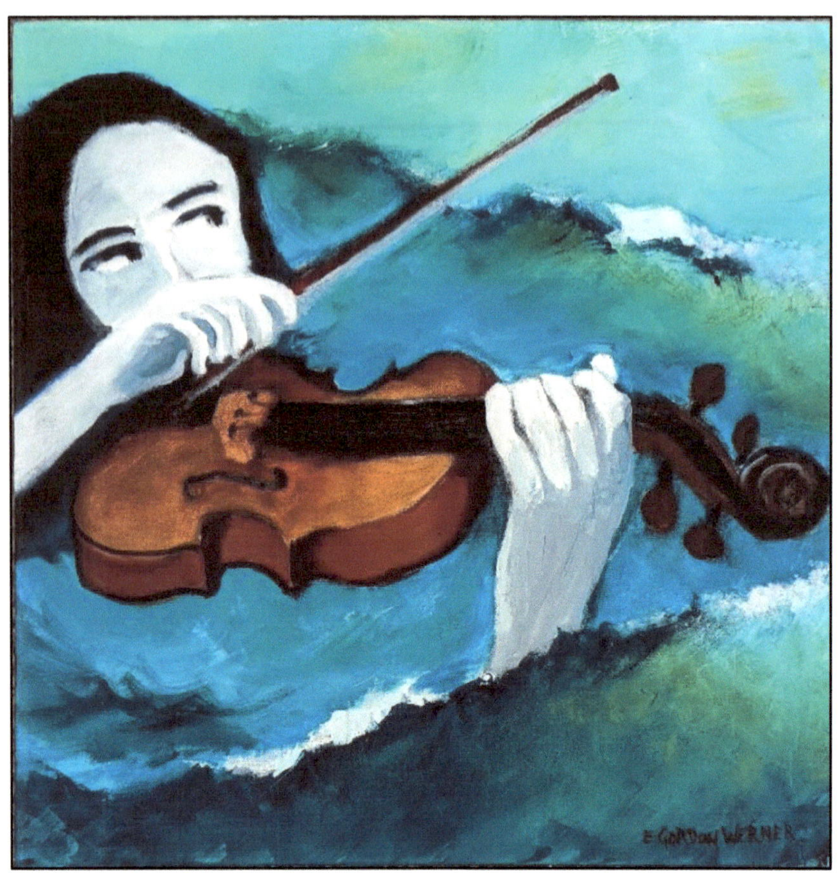

Figure 146. #3119 Violinist in rising seas. 2023 50x50 cm. Acrylic on Canvas

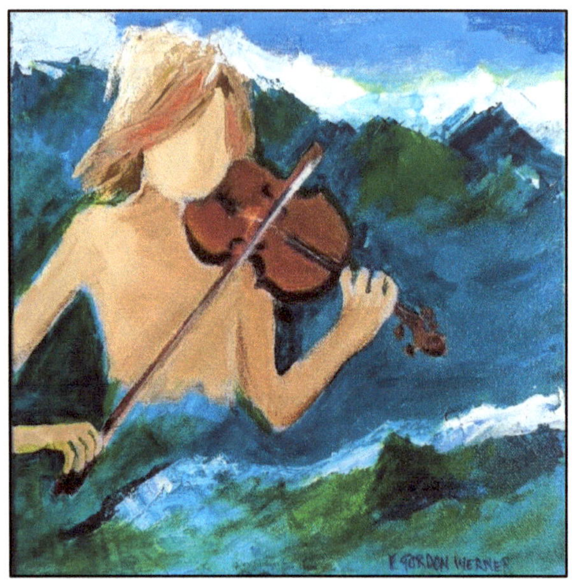

Figure 147 #3122 And then there is the next generation 2023 30x30cm Acrylic on Canvas

The artistic process remains a mystery to me. When I start a painting I can never tell what will emerge, but I know it will be different to the painting I imagine when I begin. I have learned to trust the process and go with the flow. Musicians playing with the ACO are continuing to appear in my work. This year Ike See appeared in painting #3130.

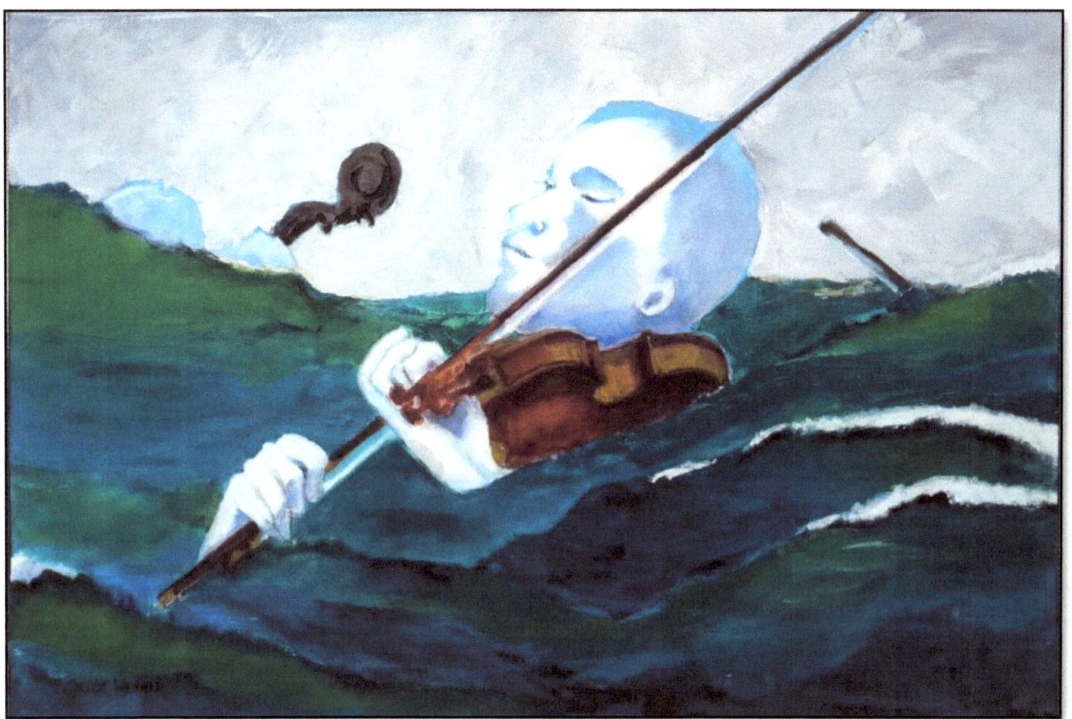

Figure 149 #3130 Violinist in rising waters. 2024 50x76cm. Acrylic on Canvas.

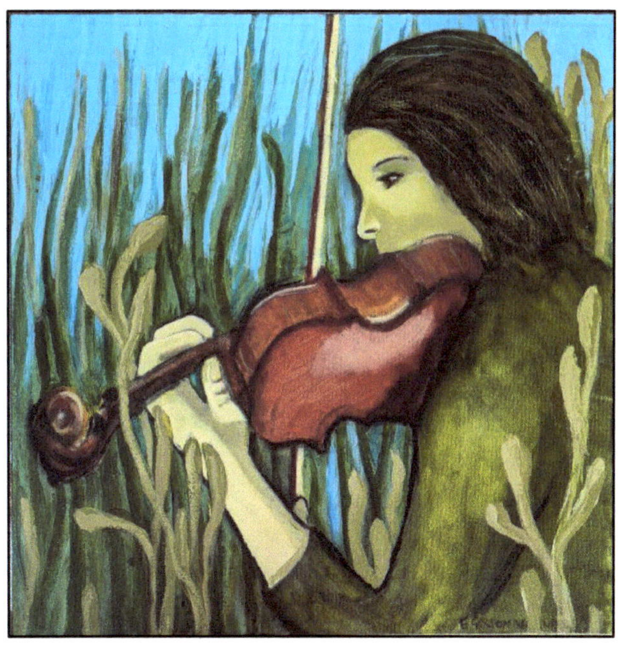

Figure 148. #3128 Underwater violinist 51x51 cm Acrylic on Canvas

The End

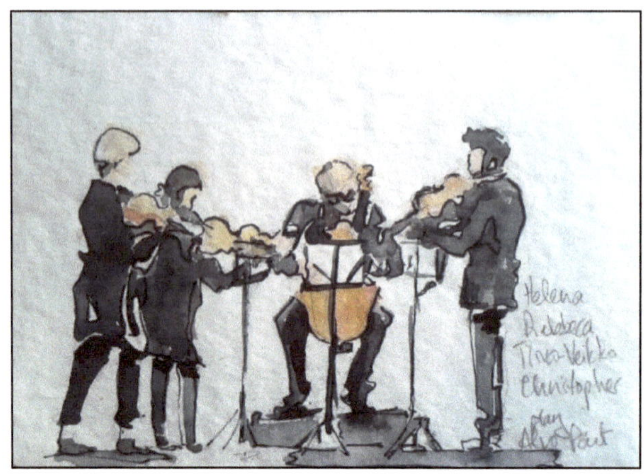

Figure 151 #2703 Playing Alvo Pärt. 2014. 12x17 Watercolour.

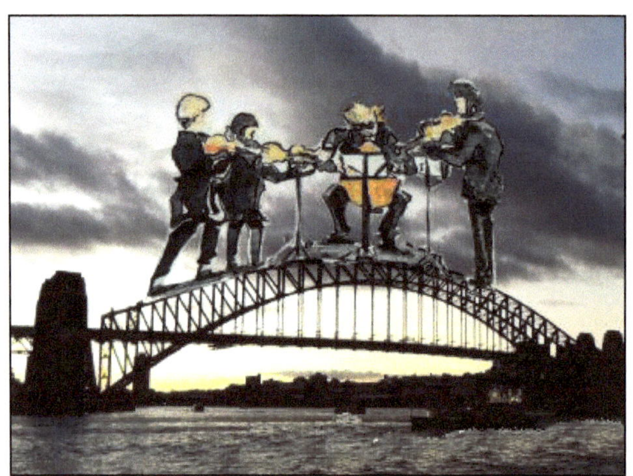

Figure 150 #2703b Playing on the Sydney Harbour Bridge. Digital Image.

Author Bio

E Gordon-Werner is a biologist (Doctorate of Natural Sciences from the University of Hamburg), artist (enrolled at Otago Art School as a mature aged student) and author. The artist's website is at www.artsmitten.com

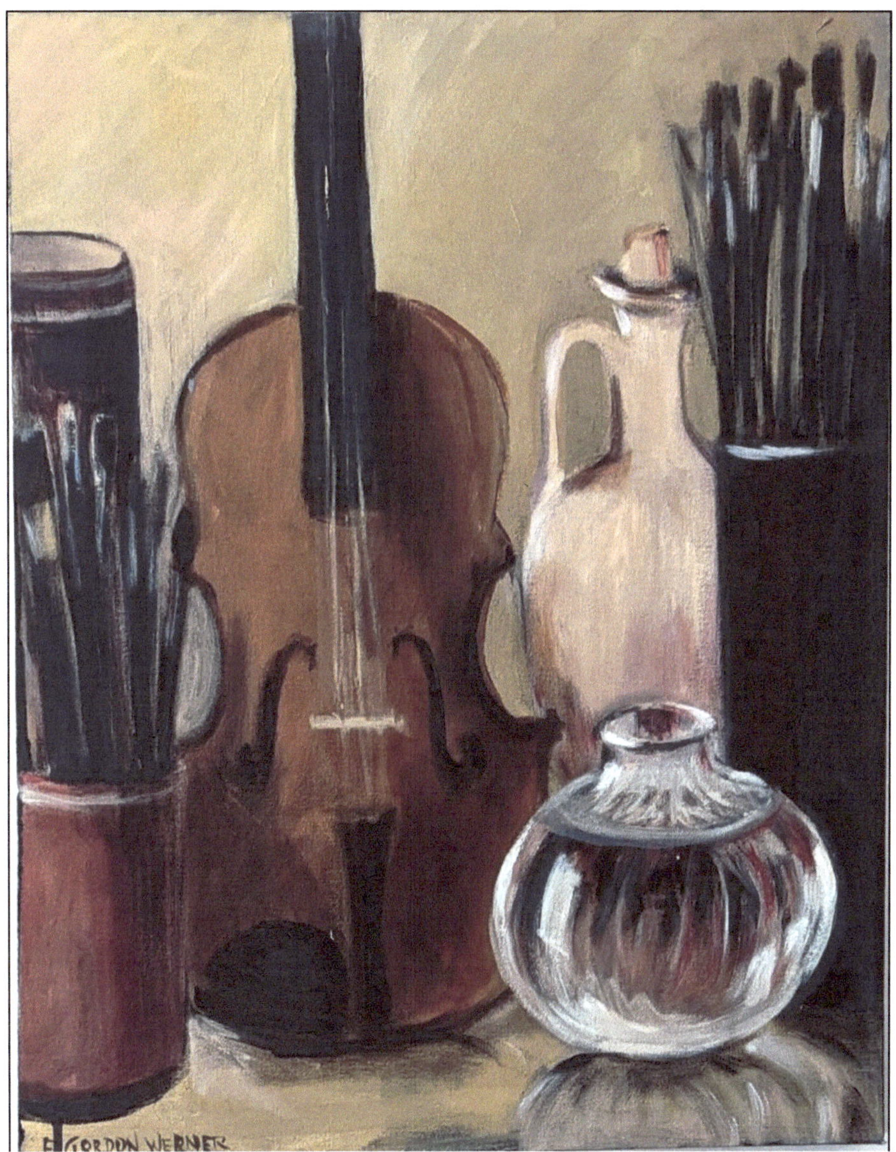

Figure 152 # 3082 Still Life with Violin. 2018. 40x50cm Acrylic on Canvas.

www.ingramcontent.com/pod-product-compliance
Lightning Source LLC
LaVergne TN
LVHW070221110826
845147LV00003B/615